MW01687847

# MESSING WITH THE CRUISE CONTROL

## A Personal History of Manic-Depression

Eric Krueger

PublishAmerica
Baltimore

© 2010 by Eric Krueger.
All rights reserved. No part of this book may be reproduced, stored in a retrieval system or transmitted in any form or by any means without the prior written permission of the publishers, except by a reviewer who may quote brief passages in a review to be printed in a newspaper, magazine or journal.

First printing

PublishAmerica has allowed this work to remain exactly as the author intended, verbatim, without editorial input.

Hardcover 978-1-4512-1243-3
Softcover 978-1-4512-1350-8
PUBLISHED BY PUBLISHAMERICA, LLLP
www.publishamerica.com
Baltimore

Printed in the United States of America

Dedicated to my sister Ellen, who stuck with me always.
And to all those people who inhabit, endure and are trying to surmount the painful world of their madness.

# Acknowledgments

I first off want to thank Jim and Jan Weiss for being the best friends and teachers anyone could want.

Thanks also to my friends and neighbors: most notably novelist Mike Goscinski, who will be on Oprah one day and has helped me no-end with my writing; Melissa Davidson for her terrific sense of humor, constant kindness and innate intelligence; Sandy Baeza, who generously fed and funded me when I was broke; John Renteria, who talked with me about everything; Wendy, an ebullient, kind, self-proclaimed Jesus-freak who often prayed for me; May Lee Lee, our superb apartment-complex manager, and Manuel Pena, our maintenance chief, who together have made life here so livable.

And for their kindness, for their simply being around, I thank all the people I know and talk with on the sidewalks of what I call my neighborhood's "Hot Zone," plus all the strangers who respond to my nod or smile or "Good morning" or "Buenos dias" or "Sup" (street talk for "Hey man, what's up?" and variations thereof)—strangers who most always make me feel good, feel some nanosecond of connection to another human being.

My apartment complex, Granada Apartments, sits in what some of us tenants affectionately call "The Ghetto." We use this term because our low-income neighborhood—in otherwise white, well-off Clovis, California (next to Fresno—midway between Los Angeles and San

Francisco) has an extraordinarily high degree and density of races, ethnic groups, crazy-medicated-functional people like me and somewhat dysfunctional but truly nice people whose brains are simply on a frequency different from that shared by most other people. With rare exceptions, we all live in peace and often friendship with each other, which I very much like.

That noted, I must add my warm special thanks to the many loved and loving people who kept me in their lives for as long as they could deal with me, most especially, David Gash, Maggie Jones, Mitchell Landsberg and Mary MacVean, and, of course, Donna Martin.

Yet another roll-call of my gratitude includes the lasting people in my life who accepted, and in some cases, nurtured me until, as is my nature, I dropped them from my life: Professor-friends Colin Atkinson, Al LaValley, Ron Gottesman, Stephen Mamber, Dave Leverenz; friends Sherry Remez, Monika DeVries, Paul Feinberg, Kevin Keegan, Curt and Terri Page, Roberta Michaeles, Jim Stratton and Susan Seagull.

And my special thanks as well to Carolyn M. Sakauye, M.D., the ophthalmologist who last year, with extraordinary surgical skill, medical experience, intellect and humor, restored vision to my left eye, which an infection had blinded.

Thanks as well to Dr. Gilbert Dale, the best urologist any guy could hope for. And to Rod and Judy Mar, my former pharmacists, and to Darren and Shelley Lew, my current pharmacists, and to Kelley, their assistant, for so humanizing their profession.

Finally, my profound thanks to June Bragg, for so many years of love and support.

And to my father, a professor of English for 45 years, who, despite our lifelong failure to love each other, has nonetheless helped me financially for years because he thinks I'm a good writer. Which, coming from him, is an honor.

# Author's Note

Memory and hindsight, in my case at least, are rarely 20/20. But a host of people over the years have told me my memory is quite good. I've come to agree with them, and have thus trusted it for much of this book.

I've also relied on, albeit with caution, the reams of anecdotal evidence I've heard from my relatives over the past 45 years.

For backup, I've used the personal journal I kept from 1967 to 1970 (1,316 pages), along with my legal documents, poems, research papers, letters, essays and newspaper work dating back to my teens. Other reminders are the hundreds of photos I have of myself and of the many people I've known from my early childhood on.

Finally, every person, place and event—everything—I've written about in this book is true; all this stuff actually happened in real time and space. However, to avoid hurting people, and to protect myself from idiot libel suits, I've changed the names of almost all the people I mention. At the same time, I've decided to run the risk of using the real names of the universities I attended, the hospitals and jails I spent time in, and certain employers I once wrote for.

Oh, and for what it's worth, I'm writing this at age 58 and have been a professional writer in California, when not manic or depressed, since 1975 (newspaper, public relations, advertising, academic, miscellany).

In turn, I've used my work experience to make this book what my trade calls "a fast, easy read."

o o o

I am not a psychiatrist (though in my next life I plan to be one), so if you want the latest, authoritative, psychiatric lowdown on manic-depression and mental disorders in general, check a good library or the Internet, and try to talk with both mental-healthcare professionals and, most especially, with crazy people.

Indeed, many people diagnosed with serious mental illness can often articulate what's going on with them. All you have to do is listen; most so-called normal people don't want to take the time, or for no concrete reason are scared to, or simply don't care.

That's too bad because first of all, most crazy people, despite their pain, are benign; and, secondly, they're often creative or well-educated or compassionate human beings, or all of these and more. And contrary to popular literature, TV and film, less than .0001% will try to kill you or eat you (however I concede the world does have a certain population of Charles Manson types who will try to kill you, and Jeffrey Dahmer types who will try to eat you for dinner, and folks like the father in Alabama recently arrested on charges of murdering his four young children by throwing them off a bridge into a river).

At any rate, my own reading about manic-depression and general psychiatry isn't bad for a layman, I think. It includes some of Google's 2,140,000 entries for "bipolar disorder" as of August 2007—along with a fine booklet called "Bipolar Disorder," published in 2001 by the National Institute of Mental Health and reprinted in 2009. I've also read and highly recommend some arguably dated but awfully good books like *Moodswing* by Ronald Fieve, M.D.; *Sanity, Madness and the Family* by Dr. R. D. Laing and Dr. A. Esterson; *Scripts People Live* by Claude Steiner, Ph.D.; *Gestalt Therapy Verbatim* by Fritz Pearls,

M.D., Ph.D.; and a number of books by Sigmund Freud, who for me is the genius-father of modern psychoanalysis, and who, though way off the mark at times, is nonetheless instructive and fascinating.

I've also read actress Patty Duke's account of her manic-depressive life, and author William Styron's description of his collision with major depression. Both are worth a look, as are other personal histories of the illness.

On TV, I once caught CNN's Larry King doing sad, revelatory interviews with broadcast journalist Mike Wallace and actor Rod Steiger about their vertical descents into depression. Moreover, I some time ago devoured a superb TV documentary about madness, on PBS I think, that highlighted a young man, a diagnosed manic-depressive who was stable thanks to good psychiatry and who'd himself become a psychiatrist to help people with mental disorders. I thought him remarkable.

*"When a child, a child of any age...can't get love, it takes what it can get, any way it can."*

Sean Connery to Tippi Hedren in Hitchcock's 1964 film, *Marnie*

# THIS WAS NO BRONSON MOVIE

I spent many of my Saturdays in 1976 at a big outdoor firing range way out in the northwest San Fernando Valley of Los Angeles. The other shooters were firing small stuff, .22s and .38s; I was blasting away with my mint-condition Colt .45 semiautomatic pistol, a cannon by comparison and a true man-stopper.

The other shooters were firing at bull's-eye targets; I used an FBI human-silhouette target. All the other shooters aimed carefully, and slowly squeezed off their rounds. I practiced quick-draw-rapid-fire (you don't aim, you point, empty your magazine fast). The range had a big sign saying you weren't allowed to do this; I ignored the sign. No one bothered me.

While firing, I fantasized the other shooters were looking at me, at once admiring me and scared of me; I felt so tough, cool and manly.

Looking back, my state of mind at the firing range was pretty sick.

o o o

In early 1977 I drove to my favorite gun store in West Los Angeles, where I placed an order for an AR-15, the semiautomatic civilian version of the U.S. military's M-16 rifle. Although I somehow never completed the purchase, I'm now wondering what was I planning to do with an AR-15? Pull another massacre like Columbine? How about Virginia Tech?

o o o

Remember the Tate-LaBianca murders of 1969? How four members of Charles Manson's psychotic cult fatally stabbed or shot five people in Benedict Canyon, Los Angeles—one of the murder victims was actress Sharon Tate, who was eight months pregnant. Remember the next night when six of these same monsters stabbed Leno and Rosemary Bianca to death in their Los Feliz district home?

I'd followed this unspeakably gruesome case in a state of fear and rage, hating cult-leader Manson as an avatar of Nazi male authority and control, inherently toxic, evil, mad, lethal.

On a conscious, albeit deranged and paranoid level, I wanted to avenge the Tate-La Bianca murders. In my unconscious mind, I think, was my wish to kill all the males who'd ever in any way hurt me.

This is why at 3 a.m. in my Los Angeles apartment, 1976, at age 26, I slid seven hollow-point bullets into the magazine of my Colt .45. Then I pulled back the slide. This loaded a live round into the pistol's firing chamber.

I slipped the weapon into my Bianchi quick-draw shoulder-holster and put on my large Army-surplus jacket.

I left my place and started walking around my normally quiet neighborhood. I hoped some thugs—better yet, some Manson-types—would jump me so I could blow them away.

No Manson-types, no desperate junkies, no demons of any kind. The streets were empty. After an hour of failing to lure attackers, I went home. Disappointed.

During this search-and-destroy mission, I saw a movie running and rerunning on the flat-screen in my head. In it I spot a big guy beating and raping a beautiful woman: I empty my magazine into the attacker's head, the hollow-points, as designed, mushroom on impact and the head explodes. Cops roll up and call me a hero. The woman falls in love with me.

o o o

This armed patrol was only one of several times when, between 1975 and 1977, I carried a loaded, concealed semiautomatic pistol into a public place, like the Beverly Hills restaurant where I met a woman for drinks; the West Hollywood fast-food place where I ate a hamburger alone; the campus of UCLA where I was a Ph.D. student; the bar just off that campus where I drank double-Beefeater gin-and-tonics; and probably more places I don't remember.

Point is: My carrying loaded guns around in public was symptomatic of homicidal paranoia—meaning I was suffering from delusions of grandeur mixed with delusions of persecution. You see, because I'm so truly great, bad people are always out to kill me.

o o o

My potentially lethal paranoia, plus a raft of other crazed feelings and behaviors, signal one extreme side of my madness: mania.

Mania is the flip side of depression. Together, these two psychiatric states form a severe mental illness called "manic-depression."

Some mental-healthcare professionals call my insanity "bipolar disorder," saying this term is neutral and thus saves patients from the negative, stigmatic label of "manic-depression."

I'll stick with "manic-depression"; it sounds its meaning: super-highs and super-lows.

And in the meantime, please keep in mind this mental illness can come with a spate of related and completely unrelated neuroses (psychosocial problems), such as chronic anxiety, sick learned behaviors and phobias.

That said, consider this: According to the National Institute of Mental Health, manic-depression currently cripples at least six million people in the United States. The number of undiagnosed people in the U.S. isn't known, and I've never seen a figure for manic-depressives worldwide, although it's probably in the tens of millions.

Whatever the exact numbers, I have a 42-year history of diagnosed, clinical (major, medical) manic-depression. Fact is, I should be dead or in a mental hospital or in jail, but instead I've written this history of my lifelong struggle with this illness and the ton of psycho-garbage that happened to come with it.

My story is for all of the people caught in the gravitational pull, the riptides and wind shears of manic-depression. I try, in my account, to offer useful information and possibly some relief, maybe a few laughs. And I think the jagged narrative of my highs, lows and mixed-states, and the psychosocial, legal and financial mess weaving through them, will do some good.

If you are struggling with my kind of madness, my story may give you some greater understanding of what you're grappling with, and, I hope, may help you find the right psychiatrist and the right medications. My story, moreover, may help you achieve a fairly stable life, at once loving, creative and productive—enriching you and those who care about you.

At the same time, what I have to say might improve your everyday life if you're among the countless, relatively sane people who knowingly or not have to cope with manic-depressives—all the family members, lovers, friends, employers, coworkers , strangers—all the people manic-depressives confuse, baffle, frustrate, anger, sadden, scare, threaten, terrify.

I know other people have written about their fights with this awful disorder. However, as a popular TV show once said, "There are eight million stories in The Naked City... "

So please stay tuned. And please forgive my at times digressing from the traditional, linear, narrative structure of most personal histories; I do so when I know I must give you certain kinds of information to help you better understand manic-depression, various neuroses and why I thought and did the crazy things I did.

# GARBLED TRANSMISSION

I recently heard someone say, "Genes load the gun. Environment pulls the trigger."

My parents always told me I was a "happy baby."They didn't know on May 22, 1950, when I was born in Newark, N.J., that at some point between my conception and delivery, nature had fucked-up.

That is, for whatever reason or no reason, nature had mangled some critical strands of my DNA—specifically those bits of genetic information responsible for the electrochemistry of my brain.

A psychiatrist 20 years later told me I had a "genetic predisposition" for a severe mental illness called "manic-depression."

Translation: Abnormally long periods of extreme elation, energy, activity, insomnia, high-speed metabolism, weight loss, hypersonic thinking, pressured speech, high affect, distractibility, anti-authoritarian behavior, charisma, narcissism, paranoia, ravenous libido, delusion, rage, extremely dangerous behavior, flat-out madness and homicidal tendencies—all of this manic stuff slowly or rapidly alternating with abnormally long periods of extreme anxiety, lethargy, sleep-addiction, weight loss or gain, flat affect, pleasing behavior, comatose libido, paranoia, sadness, terror, despair, self-hate, suicidal thinking and in some cases suicide.

Mania is up. Depression is down.

Mania is depression in reverse. Depression is mania in reverse.

One drives you into the other: a never-ending, always worsening cycle of ups and downs.

With weird transitional periods called "mixed-states," where you're going up and down at the same time—like being in an elevator that's simultaneously rising and falling at ever-changing speeds with the lights, music and your fellow-passengers fading in and out.

Indeed, until three years ago when a good shrink changed my medications, I never had any "midpoints" or intervals of what we'd agree on as stability and sanity.

No, I have always been swirling, slowly or at high-velocity, from a mixed-state to the top of Mount Everest or to the bottom of an abandoned mineshaft.

Furthermore, when I'm manic or depressed or in transit, my perceptions, intuitions and thinking are off, scrambled, twisted. I lose all connections to all people and to what most of us would say is empirical reality.

And this I can't stress enough: Along with my brain-chemical trash, I walk around with a host of neuroses not linked to brain chemicals or genes. These neuroses, these personality disorders fuel—and in turn are fueled by—my manias and depression.

Among my neuroses is "transference."This means viewing people not as they really are, but rather, viewing them as someone else entirely. In my case, to one degree or another, I perceive every adult male in my life as I did my actual father while I was growing up; my consequent behavior with this imagined father is either a constant child-like effort to please him and win his love, or total hatred and rebellion. Likewise I do mother transference.

My psychological junk also includes nonstop "projection."This is where I pin my own feelings and thoughts onto you. For example, I say to you, "You're angry at me." When the truth is, I'm angry at you.

Plus I have variously suffered from chronic anxiety, chronic sleep disorders, compulsion-obsession, social-anxiety disorder, seasonal-affective disorder, and addictions to firearms, knives, alcohol, reckless driving, sex, gambling, food and sleep.

Ultimately, you can become addicted to your own mania or depression or mixed-state. This, I believe, is the worst condition of all because you are stuck in your illness; you are immune to psychotherapy and often able to defy the most potent brain medications.

When I'm at the zenith of my mania, I'm in love with myself; I think I'm perfectly sane and the world crazy.

When I'm depressed to the point of near-total dysfunction, I hate myself; I think everyone else is stable, productive and happy. I'm the only sick one, and I am certain everyone who comes in contact with me with despises me.

In either state, I am several light years from even the fringe of what we might call sanity.

Nonetheless, and for years at a time, I have escaped my madness, or at least fought it to standstill, thanks to a few excellent psychiatrists and the meds (medications) they deemed best for me, and thanks to all the good people—relatives, friends, colleagues, neighbors, classmates—who stuck with me for as long as they could, that is, until they realized I was driving them crazy.

o o o

The word "shrink" is my shorthand for any mental-healthcare professional—from social workers to psychiatrists—who has ever treated me, or whose research I've studied.

Although most of my shrinks over the past 38 years have been either egregious mediocrities or in some cases guilty of criminal malpractice, I have known a few wise ones. Like the psychoanalyst who once told me every suicide is a potential homicide, every homicide a potential suicide. I agree. And the one who told me the end-point of my illness could be my death. I know he's right, and yet I think manic-depressives like me have a strong "life force," a crazed-determined will to live no matter what.

As for my particular form of manic-depression, I am convinced it is far more complex than most of my shrinks have realized. To help you through it, I will try to share with you my story and what I've learned from it and from good books written by smart people.

Maybe I can help you or someone you care about. Maybe I can help you spot the red flags madness most always throws up well in advance of its final onslaught. Maybe I can help you or someone you care about not decompose into another rampage shooter at place like Virginia Tech and so many elsewheres. Maybe not.

o o o

So my insanity was "inherited," genetic in origin. Well, who were my donors? For starters, I believe one standout among many was my paternal grandfather, Irwin, who died before I was born.

Despite my never knowing Irwin, I believe he had severe mental problems. To him, the laws of gravity did not apply: He was much too high much too often.

And largely because of this, his eldest son, my father, reportedly hated him; although to me my father over some 50 years only rarely and only dismissively even mentioned the guy.

Whenever I pressed him on the subject, he defaulted to denial, asserting Irwin had been normal, hard-working, gregarious and popular. Only once, when I was 57 and pressing him again, did my father slip, noting Irwin was "childlike," and "enjoyed his wine" and was, well, you know, "eccentric."

I think not.

That's because a mass of anecdotal evidence from people who knew Irwin clearly shows a man suffering from a variant of manic-depression, which shrinks might term "recurrent unipolar mania." Mania without depression. As if he were a world-class pole-vaulter who over and over again tops the bar and stays way up there for months at a time.

Worse still, and like me and other people during manias, Irwin was an alcoholic; and, like me I think, he also endured all sorts of other mental problems flying through his mind like bats on crystal meth.

So Irwin was insane. So too, I suspect, were several members of the ancestral, extended Jewish family he and I share, people who for untold centuries, via DNA, transmitted manic-depression, its variants and who knows what other madness from one generation to another in Germany and Poland and continued to do so after coming through Ellis Island circa 1903 and settling in or near Newark, New Jersey.

When or why the madness started I don't know. But I am convinced it was and is in place—often hiding, always evolving, metastasizing.

A marquee example of this was my father's uncle Louie. Still living when I was a little boy, Louie was unhappily married to a reputedly "eccentric" woman (in fact, she was bonkers) who made his life unbearable. He solved this problem by spending the bulk of each day hiding from her in a tiny workshop he'd built in a corner of their home's basement.

When my father introduced me to Louie, the man silently welcomed me with a frozen, demented smile and half-shut eyes. My father told me Louie was a furrier and liked to work alone in the basement. I remember seeing hides, tools, desultory weird stuff. I was only a kid, but I sensed something was dreadfully wrong with that man in the basement.

Another example of my mentally disordered family is my mother. She for years silently suffered from a murderous variant of manic-depression called "recurrent unipolar depression." You're like a deep-sea diver who periodically goes from the surface to the bottom, stays there much too long, eventually returns to the surface, but sooner or later dives down again, each dive deeper and longer than the last.

When I was a teenager and could clearly see my mother was in some kind of serious emotional trouble and would ask my father about her, he would, despite his knowing what was wrong, never tell me, and instead mumble some nonsense like, "She's not feeling well these days."

But he couldn't hide the facts forever—especially when I one day watched him, without a word to me, carry her limp body in a blanket down our front steps to the car, and, I later learned, drive her an hour away to the Carrier Clinic, a supposedly elite mental hospital where psychiatrists treated her with several rounds of ECT (electroconvulsive therapy), better known as "shock therapy." Translation: They strapped her to a table, anesthetized her and then zapped her brain with up to 400 volts of electricity, which threw her into what's best described as an ultra-violent seizure.

A shrink later told me this treatment often relieved major depression. He said no one knew precisely how it worked, but it was like "erasing a blackboard."

Between all the ECT and all sorts of medications, my mother to me seemed virtually flat-affect, that is, showing no emotion, zombified. This state later mixed with some of her long-standing psychological problems, and she ultimately suffered a lethal stroke.

I am reasonably sure I am far from alone in believing the mind and body are one. And thus I believe my mother's chronic mental illness killed her. In essence, then, she killed herself.

# FOR THE DEFENSE

Funny. We make people get driver's licenses, building permits, pass all kinds of tests to get all kinds of jobs—but any two idiots can bring human beings into the world and claim to be good parents when in fact they are creating madness and monsters.

My father, on every psychological front imaginable, was woefully unequipped to have a child, in this case me. And I am fairly certain that he unconsciously never wanted to have and rear children. I'm not even sure he wanted to get married: A good-looking, intelligent, gregarious, fun-loving guy, he would have been happier, I suspect, staying single for life and having one long or short love affair after another (serial monogamy without the weddings).

But no, he did what so many young Americans returning from World War II did: got a job, got married, had kids, bought a nice new suburban home, and worked his ass off to support his family.

For sure, he was always a great provider, but that granted, he was love-impaired. He had no positive parenting skills and was woefully lacking when it came to affection, tenderness and emotional nurturing—when it came to having a healthy love for his family and, most important, for himself

Remember: My father was the product of a loveless, joyless mother, and Irwin, a unipolar-manic alcoholic who neither knew nor loved him. No wonder he hated Irwin: The guy was too sick to even comprehend, let alone take on, the responsibilities of marriage and family. He was off in his own solar system, reportedly singing in the streets, throwing coins to kids, hanging out at the local police station, and often doing really crazy things like so utterly disrupting a family wedding party the guests had to throw him out.

o o o

My sister Ellen strongly disagrees with the failing parental grades I give my father. She reminds me that while she and I were growing up he worked long and hard to guarantee our food, shelter (our comfortable subdivision home in Springfield, N.J. had lawns, trees, flower beds and a nearby forest), clothing, healthcare, education and an exposure to theatre, art and literature few of our peers ever enjoyed.

This is true. He certainly had his strong points; but love wasn't one of them; and given his upbringing, he probably had a wad of unresolved, conscious and unconscious inner conflicts, terrors, regrets, anger and sadness.

This applies to many parents I've known, but I am not here to discuss their problems. And I am certainly not here to exonerate my father or pity his pain.

No. Here I am trying to tell you my story, and a huge part of that involves my father's sick parenting. So please stay with me, if you can. This isn't easy.

Especially because, as my sister notes, he did such a remarkably good job at nourishing my intellect and my appreciation for the arts while I was growing up.

Indeed, unlike my friends' parents, he turned me on in my preteens to reading excellent books and magazines. In our home, the downstairs "recreation room" (aka "TV room") was his home office. And lining one of its long walls, were equally long shelves filled with, for young me, a dazzling collection of books—classic and contemporary novels, plays, histories, biographies—a roll call including, Shakespeare, Thomas Mann, Eugene O'Neill, William L. Shirer, August Strindberg, John Updike, Eric Bently, Sigmund Freud, William Styron, Robert Brustein and so many other dynamite authors, playwrights and critics.

I called these shelves his "library," and it sparked my lifelong passion for reading and writing. As a kid and a teenager, I frequently went downstairs to browse my father's books, most always taking one up to my bedroom and reading it.

Upstairs from the library was our living room, where I'd find and read copies of *The New Yorker* magazine and *The New York Times* and lavish exhibition publications from New York City's Museum of Modern Art.

My parents were members of the museum and more times than I can remember took my young sister and me to see its collection and whatever new exhibition it was running (I still remember special showings of Joseph Turner, Diane Arbus, Andy Warhol, "Optical Art"). In addition, my sister and I got to see all kind of films the museum screened (like Orson Welles's *The Trial* and subtitled foreign stuff).

And with my father's tacit encouragement I developed my still-keen interest in World War II and military history in general—and my ongoing interest in politics and economics: I was barely 14 when I subscribed to and each week conscientiously read *U.S. News and World Report*.

What's amazing is that he never ever, unlike some parents, forced me to read anything. What he did was to create a literary environment for me to eagerly explore, appreciate and learn from.

Another wonderful gift from my father was the theater. When I was still a youngster, he often took our family to Broadway musicals, and today I can still flash back on seeing and loving hit shows like *Hello Dolly*, *Cabaret*, *Bye Bye Birdie, Golden Boy* and *Camelot*.

My super-favorite musical was *My Fair Lady*. I played the album a thousand times and read any mention of it in the *Times's* theater section. Now keep in mind my father had a weird compulsion to spring faits accompli, surprising me with things I'd never wanted or asked for. However every once in a while he'd surprise me with something neat. Prime example: He knew about my love affair with *My Fair Lady*, and one day he surprised me with two tickets for it. He later let me cut school and the two of us saw a matinee performance.

Of course I was elated all through the show; better still, my father pulled another stupendous surprise. He had without telling me written to someone connected with the production (the stage manager, I think)—and had gotten permission for the two of us to go backstage after the performance and see all the sets and meet some of the stars and watch a demonstration of the revolving, circular platform built into the stage and used, for me at least, to produce magical effects during the performance.

Funny, I recently over the phone reminded my father about our trip to *My Fair Lady*; he said he didn't remember a thing about it. That saddened me; I felt as if he'd forgotten one of the very few golden moments we ever had together.

o o o

Along with literature, modern art and theater, my father also exposed my sister and I to different cultures, sights and sounds, that is, he would take us on what might be termed "field trips." He took us, for example, to New York's Chinatown so we could experience the Chinese New Year celebration; to the city's Little Italy for the San

Gennaro street festival; to its Lower East Side to buy and eat freshly cooked yams from a street vendor; to Rockefeller Center at Christmas to see its lavish holiday lighting; to Lancaster County Pennsylvania to see the Amish; to Boston harbor to visit the historic frigate USS Constitution ("Old Ironsides); to a trolley car museum somewhere in New England; to the Christian neighborhoods near our Jewish one so we could marvel at all the blazing Christmas lights, statuettes and on one roof, a lifelike Santa about to drop down a chimney. And when I was 14 and the 1964 World's Fair opened in New York, he let me cut school and with him spend the whole day touring the fair's exhilarating pavilions.

My father also gave me the three best summers of my childhood when he took courses at Penn State University (1960), the University of New Hampshire (1961) and the University of Vermont (1962)—and he took my mother and sister with him.

These were rich summers for me, as I got to have what for youngster me were all kinds of new and exciting adventures, like exploring the beautiful university campuses; getting a small role (thanks to my father) in a university theater production; taking and enjoying summer-school classes in acting and touch-typing (again, thanks to my father).

My mother a year before her death told me these three summers were her favorites because they were the only ones "where we did things as a family." She was right.

In sum, I owe my father for much of the best education and experience of my life. For some of the best parts of who I am today.

# HOW TO DRIVE YOUR CHILD CRAZY

My father, unfortunately, in the course of teaching me good stuff, threw in a curriculum grounded in clearly sick ways of thinking, feeling and behaving.

That I appear less than happy in photos my father took when I was five is quite logical as my father's parental track record shows he was by this time practicing what one shrink told me was "physical child abuse." Indeed, he quite routinely when I was a child would accuse me of violating one of his many commandments, snarl how bad I was, grab me in one way or another and then hit me nonstop, hard with his hand or an object. I would cry and scream; I was terrified, sure he was going to kill me.

I can remember that as a child, in our pleasant, suburban home, I enjoyed no fatherly hugs, no kisses, no tenderness. What my father gave me instead were daily lectures and orders pertaining to my thinking and behavior, lectures and orders he punctuated with threats or slaps if I refused to learn and follow them. By my early teens, his incontinent prodding and bullying had taught me to be as loveless, joyless and mentally disordered as he.

Here's an example of him at work: When I barely in my teens I'd sometimes confided in him my fear, say, of failing an upcoming test at school; he'd respond by labeling and mocking me as a "worrier." Truth is, he was an alpha-dog chronic worrier, and he hated this in himself. Moreover, he was "projecting"—he unconsciously ascribed to me his own addiction to anxiety. And over time, I internalized—my mind swallowed whole—his fucking projection.

Result: By age 13, I was awash in worry. So well did I learn to worry that by my early 20s, I was often worried about being worried, and worried over that.

During this same seminal period, my father also and quite successfully taught me to embrace "tsuris" (Yiddish for "great troubles") as the meaning and purpose of life. I'm sure he learned this worldview from his mother and other relatives, and they from their ancestors, and so on back in time.

Some of my truly sane and bright immigrant relatives came to America believing it would give them a chance to prosper socially and economically. Others, however, like my paternal grandmother and her ilk, brought with them only their sorrows and terrors—their collective tsuris laced with medieval-village superstitions—and then taught them to their children, including my father, who in turn inoculated me against happiness.

This was and is at least one part of the psychology, the learned thinking and behavior that feeds and feeds off of my chemical-imbalance-induced manic-depression. Were I a shrink, I think I'd call it "psychosymbiosis."

o o o

But all this gets worse. That's because my father persistently throughout my life screws with my self-image.

Let me try to explain: The more I defy him, the more he calls me a "Rotten Kid."

On the other hand, to his friends, colleagues, the world at large, and to me if I behave, my father describes me as the brightest star in the universe. When I'm a kid, for instance, and he and my mother throw dinner parties, he summons me to the dining room, stands me in front of his guests, puts his arm on my shoulder and proudly announces: "Here is my son, Eric." At moments like these, I am his "Trophy Son."

He next peppers his guests with all my recent achievements—like the straight-A report card I just got for the last marking period; and the model space capsule I built for the school science fair; and our joint trip the week before to see a Broadway musical. While he talks, I nod and smile. He then has me flesh out his narrative and take questions from the audience.

Trotting me out this way for years—even when I was in college and home on vacation—increasingly warped me. I didn't know whether I was a terrible kid or a great kid. I was confused and angry: Which kind of kid was I?

Some shrinks might agree with me when I state my father was "double-binding" me—meaning: He for some 50 years of my life sends me two utterly contradictory messages about myself—and if I point this out, he denies it.

Enough of such mixed-messaging and denial over enough time is absolutely crazymaking: You learn to distrust and finally discard your own perceptions and intuitions about yourself and reality. You do not know who you are—no sense of self, no positive concrete identity. You let the madness of other people fill your vacuum.

Once in a while I did have some wonderful moments, virtual epiphanies, when I finally thought I knew for sure who I was and what I wanted to do with my life. But if my father disagreed with my self-assessment, as he most often did, and I held my position, he'd invariably denounce me as rotten or crazy or both.

No wonder my self-image was and is so skewed and black.

o o o

Really bad is that when all this father-gunk was streaming into my head, I couldn't run home to momma for help. Because I didn't have a mother. Sure, I lived in a house with an older woman who was my chauffeur, laundress, cook, paramedic, cleaning lady—who performed all her 1950s suburban, homemaking tasks perfectly. In the course of all this, however, she silently blared to me that she was only a wife and mother by default.

You see, her dream in high school was to become a professional actress on the stage or in film. After high school, she attended the American Academy of Dramatic Arts in Manhattan. Somewhere along the line, she suffered what might be called a crisis of self-confidence which led her to decide she didn't have the talent to make it on Broadway or in Hollywood or anywhere else. I suspect that after the Academy, after she gave up on her dream, she consciously or not felt scared, lost and lonely and thus escaped into marriage and babies and housekeeping. She apparently felt she had no other options.

That she took first-rate physical and logistical care of me is a given. But don't think for a minute she ever loved me. How could she? She couldn't love herself (just as my father couldn't love himself). Furthermore, her knowledge of parenting, of maternal nurturing—of how to grow a mentally healthy human being—was zilch.

o o o

Before major depression sidelined her, my mother only compounded my father's damaging me. Here's a fun one: When I was a kid she'd often tell me to do something, say, go downstairs to her food shelves and bring her three cans of string beans. Well, for whatever reason, I'd return with two cans of string beans and one of corn. "You never listen!" she'd shout. "You never listen!" After a few years of hearing her say this to me, I stopped listening to her altogether.

Worse still, my deafness generalized. I stopped listening to most of my teachers most of the time. I stopped listening to most everyone.

And, sadly, in my late teens, when I'd see serious plays on and off Broadway, I heard all the lines but nothing registered; I'd leave the theater unable to recall a word of the play, not really knowing what it had been about.

My mother laid another cute trip on me. When she got super-angry at me for what she deemed some gross misbehavior on my part, she didn't become a flamethrower like my father. No, she simply stopped talking to me. And if I entered a room she was in, she'd walk out. This was her "Silent Treatment."

And after enduring up to three days of her treatment, I felt like the worst kid on Earth, unworthy of anyone's love—then I felt invisible. Dead.

My mother's crazymaking punishment, and some other warped and warping behaviors, made impossible the tiniest mother-son bonding. We didn't even try to communicate until I was in my early 50s and she her late 70s. We made progress, but her death ended our efforts to connect.

o o o

As for her silent treatment: When I was 32 and living in Los Angeles and fully self-supporting, I finally got fucking sick of my parents hassling me over the phone every week from their home in New Jersey. So one day I unplugged my phone and kept it unplugged save for my outgoing calls (I also used my various work numbers for personal calls). I did this from 1982 until 1998: zero contact of any sort.

My absenting myself from my parents' lives for 16 years made them, according to my sister, alternately sad, angry, lost, confused, victimized. What had they ever done to me? they wondered.

I can infer my parents may have felt somewhat as I did as a youngster when my mother gave me her silent treatment. Only I returned it in spades.

And while child-parent estrangement isn't uncommon, my degree of vengeful "fuck-you!" rage, of not needing or wanting them for anything, of finally being free of them, was a bit higher and much more pressurized, more inflated and elongated, than that of most bitter sons and daughters, except in cases of parricide (a kid killing a parent).

All the same, I today, at age 58, still hear my parents' voices in my head. I still hear their volleys of criticism, insults and rage aimed at me; I still feel their psycho-shrapnel lodged in my brain.

Stuff like my father getting angry at 19-year-old me over some nonsense and screaming "I'll cut your balls off!"

Or the day when I was 24 and about to drive from New Jersey to Washington, D.C. and had, minutes before, adamantly refused to talk on the phone with my father's functional-psychotic mother whom he worshipped and I hated. Upshot: He furiously shouted, "So you're driving back. Good. I hope you crash and die!"

What kind of father talks to his son this way? And yet I remember countless explosions like these.

Notwithstanding my excellent medications, I can't always shake all the painful memories my parents and other toxic people have generously given me. I call these memories my "demons." The moment I fight them off, they charge right back at me, like predatory bill collectors who keep calling you back no matter how often you hang up on them.

Not surprisingly, I recently told my sister that much of my love for alcohol stems from its ability to napalm my demons, at least for a few hours.

o o o

I believe no solid correlation exists between people's professional performance and their parenting performance. My father was a superlative grade-school and high-school teacher who went on to spend nearly 45 years as a professor of English at Kean University, a large state institution in Union, New Jersey. He would have stayed longer had not a major hip fracture when he was 87 grounded him for good.

Prior to his unscheduled retirement, he'd always given the best of his himself to his students. And, according to all reports, he emblemized the consummate classroom teacher.

He also had a warm bedside manner with students who came to him with personal problems, and he had many rich relationships with colleagues—and yet none of the personality traits that made for his popularity on campus ever carried over into his household. With us he was more than not cold, selfish, pedagogic in an arrogant way, badgering, hypercritical, hostile, controlling, flat-out dictatorial and, if he didn't get his way, violent.

At the very same time, he didn't seem to know where his classroom ended and our home began. You see, most universities—and certainly Kean, even during the campus unrest of the late '60s—endow their professors with absolute academic power over students. Which is to say that within the limits of state and federal law, the professor is God in the classroom.

And I suspect my father, by virtue of his campus status and power, simply assumed he was the God of our household. He certainly tried to control virtually every thought and behavior of my mother, my sister and myself. He mostly achieved only partial victories, but that never blunted his oppressive effort.

No wonder, as well, he happily spent a number of summers as a camp counselor, lording it over young boys with the same kind of power he enjoyed at Kean.

Talk about a control-freak: I vividly remember one summer when he was a counselor at an overnight camp in Massachusetts, in charge of a cabin of boys around age nine. I was a camper in an adjacent cabin of younger kids. One day I for some reason made my first visit to my father's cabin; no one was there—but dotting the walls were paper signs he'd written in colored crayon demanding to know: "HAVE YOU HAD YOUR BOWEL MOVEMENT TODAY?"

The signs shocked and embarrassed me. Those kids had been toilet-trained years earlier and knew how and when and where to shit—and yet he's rhetorically ordering them to produce daily stool samples! Gimme a break.

o o o

My father, as I've said not only liked to control me, he liked to surprise me as well—often with disastrous consequences. Here, from the past, is a classic example of his functional madness: He one night when I was age 11 came home and presented me with a clarinet. I'd never asked for a clarinet. I'd never wanted a clarinet. Maybe a trumpet, like my buddy Ron, but never a clarinet. He didn't care about what I wanted; he didn't even hear when I objected to the instrument. No, this

Nazi hired a music teacher to tutor me at home, cursed and hit me when I refused to practice, forced me to play in the school orchestra. I hated him for all this.

In time, I got angry enough to launch a Tet Offensive against him and his fucking clarinet. One of my tactics was disrupting the twice-weekly orchestra rehearsals I loathed and had to play in; after one sabotage success, the music teacher, whom I despised, started yelling at me. In front of my fellow musicians, I gave the guy the finger—and got myself expelled from the orchestra for good.

My father gave up. The clarinet was no more.

o o o

A parallel idiocy was Hebrew school. These days my father is essentially a secular humanist, but back in 1964, following my 1963 bar mitzvah (a real joke since I'd declared myself an atheist a year earlier), he was still a practicing reform Jew and insisted I continue attending our congregation's religious school. Problem was I'd grown over time to utterly loath every Sunday morning in a cramped little classroom listening to some moron teacher carry on about how we Jews were "the chosen people" (isn't that the equivalent of what Hitler told the Germans?) and stressing the courage and nobility of our ancestors and the glory of Israel.

Along with having to hear this propaganda, we also had to contribute money each week to a private organization that helped bankroll the Israeli cause.

I so hated all of this shit (and Judaism and all religion) that I one Sunday morning barricaded myself in my bedroom and shouted to my father I was not under any circumstances going to fucking Hebrew school. He snapped into one of his physically violent rages and over and over and over again hurled his entire body against my blocked bedroom door (it had no lock). That he couldn't charge into my bedroom to beat me into attending Sunday class was because I had my upper body jammed against the door and my right leg extended backward into the wall behind me. This leveraging worked! And, finally exhausted, he gave up and went away; I left my room when I sensed he'd calmed down or had left the house.

I subsequently used this jamming technique to thwart every attempt he made to storm my room. Better still, I was within two years or so big enough and strong enough to kill him if he tried to hit me. And I would have. Perhaps he sensed this because by that time he'd given up on attempting corporal punishment—only to intensify his verbal and psychological abuse.

o o o

Around the time of my clarinet-Hebrew-school rebellion, 1964, I was 14 and increasingly disaffected with my junior high school's attempt to educate me. I stopped caring about "working up to my potential," as my teachers said I should, and was demoted from my school's elite "A Track"—the best teachers and curricula for the best students—to a "B—" track, which was fine with me.

I also got a little weird with other kids. I one day in a school hallway accused a fellow-student of stealing one of my jackets, then I shoved him up against a locker, pulled a knife and held it against his throat. A teacher grabbed me and hustled me to the principal, who called me a "hood" and said I'd never get anywhere in life.

But I since I'd excelled in all my history classes (history was the only subject I liked) and was a white Jew in a town pretty much dominated by its huge Jewish community, and since my father, after all, was well-known in that community and a much-respected professor at a nearby university—I walked.

My father, of course, privately excoriated me. He was convinced more than ever that his trophy son was now a rotten kid.

Back comes the double-bind. At roughly the same time my father was furious with me over the knife thing, among other antisocial behaviors, he was guiding me through the application process for admission to a prestigious private school for the following year. (As with the clarinet and so much other stuff, I'd never asked for this). So now I'm both his rotten son and his trophy son. I got into the place, but since it decided my father made too much money for me to get a full scholarship, my father withdrew my application. He probably could have afforded the tuition, but that's another story.

Anyway, I proceeded to war against him and my junior high school and steadily withdrew from the social life I'd earlier enjoyed with my classmates. I was clearly a troubled kid who needed help. But no one noticed.

Eighth grade finally ended. Fuck all of you, fuck everything, I'd been feeling. So the very night after my graduation ceremony—at which, get this, I was awarded a history medal from The Daughters of the American Revolution—I ran away from home. (This was a few years before running away from suburbia to Haight-Ashberry, the Lower East Side or some commune in the Arizona desert, was for many of my generation a cool thing to do.)

I didn't for some reason go alone, no, I invited a rebellious friend who hated his parents to come with me. My plan for us was to reach California and survive by working in the fields, or maybe the movie industry.

We actually made it to Chicago, but made some dumb mistakes and got caught and sent back to New Jersey, where my father kept me prisoner, forcing me to take summer school classes every morning, monitoring my afternoon work as a golf-club caddy, dragging me to summer college classes he was teaching (I read in the school library until he came for me) —and getting me to believe, and by now I did, that I had really sinned. I felt awful about myself, worthless.

And so that September, when I started high school, I felt compelled to make up for all my sins, to prove myself a good person, which I did, a bit too much.

# REDEMPTION?

*"We may never know the circuit diagram for all the electrochemical pathways within the human brain."*

Neil deGrasse Tyson, astrophysicist, *Death by Black Hole and Other Cosmic Quandaries*, 2007

"You'll never work this hard in college," my father once told me, almost sadly, past midnight, when he found me, a 14-year-old high-school freshman killing myself on a research paper about the Aztecs for an elite history class called FAC (Foundations of American Culture).

He was right. But I was too obsessed with my work—with atoning for my awful past—to hear him. I ended up handing in a 19-page, clearly A+ paper; much to my horror, the teacher, Mr. Richards, took off 13 points because I'd forgotten to put my bibliography in alphabetical order. This meant that instead of the A I wanted so badly for the marking period, I'd only get a B. Having no one to blame but me, I bitterly accepted my punishment.

Now, remember my father and the clarinet nonsense? As I said, that episode was merely one of near-countless others. My father loved pulling clandestine operations on me—surprising me, as I've described, with all sorts of stuff, faits accomplis, random cruel denials and whimsical permissions; going behind my back to help or hurt me, trick me, get even with me for some phantom crime I'd committed against him.

Please forgive my whining on about my father; despite years of psychotherapy and medication, I will probably die with my deep, father-aimed anger and sadness; I will die still searching for and never getting the love I want from him—a futile, sick effort that remains a major sinkhole in my personality, and one at bottom unrelated to my manic-depression

At any rate, after hearing me explain why I'd only be getting a B for the marking period, my father, without telling me ahead of time, paid Mr. Richards an after-school visit. I don't know what he said to my teacher, but I assume he openly or tacitly pulled rank on him—something like "I'm a university professor and I know ten times more than you about teaching and how dare you penalize my son (here I'm his trophy son) 13 points after he slaved away for weeks on this thing, and if you don't correct this matter I'll…"

Sure enough. I got an A in FAC. On hearing this, my father told me with great pride about how he'd carpet-bombed Mr. Richards. Which left me 20 times more embarrassed and ashamed than a hundred Bs. I felt like a cheat, a kid who'd used his father to get an A. When I went to FAC the next day, I couldn't face Mr. Richards, and I wondered if the others kids knew. What a fucking mess.

o o o

As with the Aztecs, I madly drove myself throughout my freshman and sophomore years to be a super-high achiever in terms of grades, honors and extracurricular activities. I behaved this way to make up for what I still believed were my past crimes and inherent worthlessness, and because I was convinced I'd never get anywhere in life without a college degree.

I really bought the college shit, already at age 14 perusing college catalogues in the school library. I also ran for freshman class president and won. The next year I won unopposed. I got into the prestigious Kiwanis Key Club and later was inducted into the elite Honor Society; best of all, I eagerly joined the debate team and the National Forensic League—moves I deemed vital to my getting into college and winning some great career.

Careers. From childhood through my early 50s, I'd lock on to a career goal for a year or two and then dump it for something else. During my first two years of high school, I wanted to be a diplomat for the U.S. State Department. I had visions of me posted in London, Paris or Berlin, wearing a gray pinstriped suit and sitting in the back of a chauffeured Rolls-Royce.

o o o

So here I am: locked into neurotic hypomania on afterburners. ("Hypomanic" is shrink talk for just below manic.) What's really sad here is that despite all my achievements, I still felt worthless, my self-image was still at best fuzzy and at worst jet black.

But back to the debate team. It was under the auspices of our school's chapter of the National Forensic League, which, along with sponsoring our formal debate competitions against teams from other schools, enabled us to compete in speechmaking, extemporaneous speaking, dramatic reading and more. I did it all. And most always won first place in whatever I did.

Manic-depressives, even incipient ones like me at this time, tend to be quite verbal and articulate, sometimes charismatic, when high. I did well in any class that required and rewarded good speaking, classes like history, English, world literature, economics.

Unfortunately, when I hit full-blown mania a few years later, I, like many manics, suffered from what shrinks call "flight of ideas and pressure of speech." I would lose control of my talking, like a driver who loses control of a car while speeding; I would hold my listeners only until they realized I was crazy. Those who didn't realize this often got sucked into my madness and sometimes joined me in acting out my twisted fantasies—although at some point everyone runs from me.

This ability to attract and then lose an audience also showed up during my major depressions. A lot of good people would spend weeks and often months trying to help me. They inevitably failed, gave up and vanished. A shrink once told me they left me because I reminded them of their own sadness. I'm not sure this is true, but I do recall a college friend, Carol, gently telling me, "I'm not going to see you anymore, Eric, because I want to laugh again."

A few people would stick with severely depressed me, but that's largely because they were, or seemed to be, oblivious to my specific condition or knew little about depression in general. Which is why when I was with them, I felt horribly alone.

# THE BIG ONE AND MEAN CUISINE

Before I tell you about my ever-growing craziness in high school and college and beyond, I feel the need to note some of my lifelong obsessions: One is military warfare, World War II in particular. The other is negative body-image, my always feeling fat and unattractive, a neurotic anxiety stemming more from environmental factors than my sick brain chemistry, but all the same affecting and affected by it.

First off: war. As a kid, I loved military conflict. Loved mock combat with my friends in the streets and woods of our neighborhood, loved my huge collection of little soldiers and vehicles which I'd divide into opposing armies and then throw into violent battles. By age 10, I was reading all kinds of military history and watching every war movie and TV war show I could.

World War II especially mesmerized me—its sheer scale and seismic violence, its guns, planes and ships. I of course identified with America, but I thought the Germans had cool uniforms and tanks. I'm not sure I'd ever heard about The Holocaust until I was eight or so and sitting in our kitchen when I heard my father call up to me from our downstairs recreation room, "Eric, come here, look at this." I sat down next to him on the sofa, and he showed me the text and photos of an official WWII U.S. military report he'd brought back from the war (he'd been in military government), and had just discovered while poking around his numerous piles of books and papers.

The report, published in 1945, was about the Nazi concentration camp Dachau. My father turned the pages very slowly: all those naked, skeletal, dead people. Every so often, he'd grimly say, "Look at this, look at what they did."

This was not the war my friends and I fought in the woods where getting killed by an imaginary opponent merely meant you had to lie on the ground and count to 20, after which you could jump back into life.

No, Dachau was real death. And all those corpses lying on the ground were, I think, the first dead people I ever saw. This spurred me to read all I could about the extermination camps, the gas chambers, the ovens, the mountains of bodies, the gold ripped from victims' teeth, the skin turned into lamp shades.

This evil and madness stunned me. And fascinated me: My father had also brought home from Germany and given me a large swastika flag, swastika armband, military document signed by Nazi king-pin Hermann Goring and more. I treasured this stuff and tacked the big swastika flag to my bedroom wall. It stayed there until our black maid complained about it to my mother, who made me take it down.

A little weird, too, was my deciding at age 11 I wanted to get a Ph.D. in modern European history and write books like William L. Shirer's monumental bestseller *The Rise and Fall of the Third Reich.*

This career thing was so desultory. I went from wanting to be a fireman to being a civil engineer and later a diplomat and during my junior year in high school I first wanted to become an actor but then fixed my sights on being an attorney in the Justice Department's anti-Mafia unit (I unconsciously saw the Mob as my father); senior year, I decided to be a writer (about what I wasn't sure, but I'd already done a lot of extracurricular writing: a play, a few short stories, poetry—most of it not terribly good, some a little crazy).

Writing. I'd gone on a letter-writing binge in my preteens. For example, I wrote a long letter to William L. Shirer saying how I'd read all his books on Nazi Germany and wanted to get a Ph.D. in history and be like him. His literary agent wrote me a long, kind response. So then I wrote to Sir Winston Churchill, saying I'd read his multivolume history of World War II (not quite true, but I was learning hyperbole, it goes with the illness); Churchill at the time was recovering from a hip fracture, and I naturally sent him my best wishes. His secretary sent me a kind, appreciative note on his official letterhead.

During this same period I also wrote to the CEO of a huge New Jersey public utility, advising him to go nuclear. Then I lettered Adlai Stevenson, our ambassador to the U.N. He died right about that time; however I did get to visit the U.S. mission to the United Nations in Manhattan. And our local newspaper published the story I wrote about my visit.

My friends and the other kids at school weren't doing this odd stuff. I was writing to all these proxy fathers I so admired and from whom I wanted what I perceived to be their love

But back to war. You see, I only now see how war mirrors manic-depression. For me and perhaps a billion other people now and back then, World War II was unambiguous, black and white. Theaters of war and campaigns and battles were either triumphs (mania) or defeats (depression) or sea-saw (mixed-states). War expressed my polarized perceptions of reality, my repressed and expressed rage and pain and concomitant obsession with violence and death.

These days I still read about World War II, enjoy war documentaries on the History Channel, and almost daily I follow Iraq. The difference is I no longer find anything cool about war; to paraphrase a rabbi I once talked with, war is a failure of humanity.

o o o

Manic-depression can cause or weave into eating disorders and disordered thinking about eating.

I have never been clinically anorexic or bulimic. But for the last 48 years, since I was about age 10, I have almost every waking day worried about my becoming overweight, fat, obese.

I clearly remember sitting next to my sixth-grade classmate, Livia, in the school cafeteria at lunch and our talking not about kid stuff but rather about dieting—about how we could lose weight by only eating hard-boiled eggs, and how we both wanted to lose weight.

After school, I'd stand in front of my mother's full-length mirror and see myself as fat and deformed, even though everyone else back then called me thin, slender or skinny (this holds true for most of my life). Point is, I was as a kid suffering from a chronic, acutely negative and false image of my body. I can't speak for Livia, but precisely why I was so obsessed so young with my weight, and later with the weight of other people, why I so feared and hated fatness, seems to have stemmed from our culture's sick obsession with weight and appearance. I'd internalized this. So did all the kids I knew—save in my case, manic-depression and neuroses would soon intensify it exponentially.

I do have one awful, telling memory from my early teens. I vividly recall the day in gym class when our coaches lined us up and one of them lectured us on the importance of being physically fit. Then they singled out Tyrone, who was borderline-obese, and told him to do sit-ups. He tried hard, struggling against his immense weight, his face red and sweaty. He gave up, not even half a sit-up. The coaches laughed at him and then insulted him for being fat. The assembled kids were silent, grim. I was in shock. And I warned myself to never ever gain weight.

From back then, I have another memory: My parents, grandparents, aunts and uncles forever telling me to eat and shoving food at me, coaxing me with "Here, have more!" They were happy when I ate. Good kids ate, good kids stuffed themselves. I know this sort of "Clean-Your-Plate" imperative is common on our planet, but I grew to dislike it intensely: Those bastards wanted to make me fat like them. I visualized Tyrone's humiliation in gym class and shuddered.

Over the many years since, during my manias, relatives and friends have variously told me I looked too thin or underweight, some said "gaunt" or like a "concentration-camp victim"—I hear this stuff and think "Great!" Or think "No you're wrong, can't you see how fat I am?"

Needless to say, the higher I got, the more I slimmed down, sometimes too much. Once when I was 25 and severely manic, a doctor told me with some urgency that I had burned up what fat I had and was now catabolizing, that is, he said, I was burning up muscle tissue. He told me to drink lots of malted milks.

I have recently heard experts say two-thirds of all Americans are either overweight or obese. I see flocks of such people every day at Wal*Mart, on the bus, on the sidewalks, everywhere. I dread becoming one of them, I dread becoming one of those middle-aged guys with a huge pot belly pushing out over my belt.

Truth is: My only overweight periods came during major depressions when I wasn't on medication. Many severely depressed people lose their appetite; not me: Whenever I joined their dejected ranks, I was always eating. That's because big, high-calorie meals and constant snacking for a few minutes relieved my hyper-anxiety and despair. Food became the only pleasure I had left—until I started hating myself for gaining weight.

These days I feel 10 pounds overweight (based on what standard I don't know). I blame Prozac, my antidepressant medication, which reportedly can screw up metabolism and cause weight gain. Every morning, I check my abdomen in the bathroom mirror before showering: No matter how straight I stand, no matter how much I suck in my gut—I think I look fat, although I'm not. Sometimes I think I look pregnant, which is ridiculous.

Meantime, I try to be careful, count my calories daily, and once in a while actually feel okay with my weight and how I imagine I look to others. I often forget that no one ever sees my body as I see it. And past a certain point, on one except me cares about my body.

# BOND, JAMES BOND

Okay, we're back in high school, my freshman and sophomore years, ages 14-16, 1964-1966. I'm clearly hypomanic and sporting all sorts of neuroses. On top of all my school hyperactivity, I'm also working various nights as an usher at what was then Symphony Hall in Newark, N.J., and when not doing that I frequently baby-sat for numerous couples in my neighborhood.

I was already getting somewhat antisocial and nonconformist. For instance, I, unlike almost every other kid in my high school, refused to attend our varsity-sports events like the sold-out Saturday football games. I hated being an insignificant part of any crowd, and thus resented all those football fans in the stands cheering for their heroic players on the field—instead of cheering for me; I resented them for not focusing all their attention and adoration on me: I unconsciously wanted love that badly, love from everyone anywhere anytime.

o o o

Meanwhile, I only had and only wanted one genuine friend. His name was Joel, he was my age and the only person who seemed to accept me and to a degree share with me my fantasies—especially my desire to be James Bond.

I had already read most of Ian Fleming's popular spy thrillers about James Bond, the British secret service agent 007 who was "licensed to kill." And with Joel I saw the Bond films the week they came out. Now Joel and countless other boys (and men) may have variously and understandably identified with Bond: He was handsome, suave, brave, well-built, well-educated; he knew wine and cards and martial-arts, he carried a Walther PPK in a neat shoulder-holster, he got to make love with the most gorgeous women on Earth.

My problem here is that I, as they say, went overboard. To an arguably psychotic degree, I by this point in my life secretly saw myself as a puny, unmanly smudge of nothing. So, logically, I dreamed of replacing myself with James Bond, and made him my God.

I don't remember how but during this period I bought a super-cool, semiautomatic $CO_2$ pellet pistol (lethal), and from an army-surplus store bought a shoulder-holster to carry it, concealed. I also bought a tiny tape recorder and with Joel, in his basement, hid the device inside an attaché case—modeled directly after the super-weapon attaché case Bond carries in *From Russia with Love*. We also found a way to hide in the case a throwing knife and other spy weapons and gadgets.

Not long after the attaché case and related projects, I one night by accident, with one shot from my pellet pistol, blew out the rear windshield of the Bernsteins' (my next-door neighbors) Ford Falcon. If the car had "safety glass" the shit didn't work; a thousand tiny shards flew everywhere. And I snapped back into my terrified-child-post-Chicago sense of having sinned. I ran crying into the Bernsteins' house, confessed to my criminal act, promised to pay for a new windshield and begged for their forgiveness. Mr. and Mrs. Bernstein were pissed but nice. And the next day I did pay them for the damage; I also got Joel to take permanent ownership of the pistol. I only wanted to return to being a good boy and an A student.

o o o

The rest of the year was largely uneventful, with the exception of one pivotal disclosure from my father. He and my mother had vacationed on an island the summer before. And without consulting me—his control-freak-secrecy mentality at work—he had met the owner of the Nobska Playhouse, a small summer theater on this island and had arranged with him for me to be an apprentice (student actor-technician) at the theater for the summer following my sophomore year.

This was stupendous. Remember, my love for the theater went back to my grade-school years and now I was not only getting a chance to work in one—but for the first time I was going to be far from home and completely on my own. Instead of the summer camp I would have normally gone to, I'd have for the first time my own rented room and get to eat every meal in coffee shops and like an adult do my own laundry. Best of all, I'd be out of my father's immediate, suffocating reach.

# STAGESTRUCK

The name of the place was Nantucket. I'd never been anywhere like it: a 48-square-mile island 30 miles off the coast of Massachusetts. For someone like me at 16, someone slowly but surely rolling into the chaos of manic-depression, Nantucket—with its perfectly preserved Colonial and 19$^{th}$-century architecture, its calm daily rhythmic flow of tourists mixed with its well-heeled summer residents and year-round natives, its rain-rippled fog, tawny-green moors and windy beaches—for someone like me, Nantucket that summer of 1966, despite all my projection and paranoia, gave me the most inner peace and happiness I'd ever known.

When not working or taking an acting class at Nobska Playhouse, I often spent time with Ken and Beatrice Tyler, who, in their 50s and from Illinois, summered at their splendid wood-and-glass home in the middle of the island's moors. They talked to me as if I were an adult. And maybe most important, they never put me down.

Ken was a professor of English and drama who'd volunteered to direct a play the Nobska was going to present, a play that needed a teenaged boy for one of its leading roles. Ken chose me for the part; he taught and coached and drilled me to act; and I had a deliriously happy, heady week playing a character on a stage in front of an audience, and feeling ineffably high at curtain call, soaking up that wonderful applause, which I craved.

Offstage, I enjoyed and admired Ken: Along with his being a Yale Ph.D. scholar, he was an ex-Navy officer and a big, manly outdoors type. On a deeper level, I loved his warmth, wisdom and emotional honesty, and most of all his ability to give and accept love with such extraordinary ease—he really was that kind of complete human being. And, of course, in my misdirected, love-starved mind, he was the perfect father. As I noted earlier, manic-depressives like me see other people and most other aspects of reality in black and white. Even today, despite good medication and good therapy, my perceiving life in shades of gray is always very hard. I note this because although I have just painted Ken as a god, I have to remind myself that, no, he was a human being, with all the flaws and frailties, regrets and demons any one of us is prone to.

o o o

My sensational summer ended in early September when I returned to Springfield and kicked-off my junior year in high school, 1966-1967, feeling what I took to be self-worth and a palpable sense of who I was and what I wanted from life.

I now wanted to be a professional actor. I enrolled in Saturday acting classes at a prestigious studio in Greenwich Village and dreamed of going to the Yale School of Drama. I secretly wanted to be a star, that is, until, like my mother decades earlier, I eventually decided I didn't have enough talent to be a successful actor on the stage, the screen or anywhere else.

o o o

*"...the test of a first-rate intelligence is the ability to hold two opposed ideas in the mind at the same time, and still retain the ability to function."*

F. Scott Fitzgerald, "The Crack-Up," 1936.

As my junior year progressed, my inchoate manic-depression and other mental fuck-ups slowly eclipsed the inner glow of my first Nantucket summer, landing me in a mixed-state (the disordered condition I mentioned earlier, the one where you're going up and down at the same time).

My mental tumbles grew steadily in frequency and intensity, and by June 1967, I was more troubled than I and others realized. Here's an example, drawn from the piles of my published and unpublished writing since high school—the writing I preserve to prod myself to remember the productive, intelligent, creative best of me. These words, however, are clear markers of disturbance. I excerpted them from an essay we had to write for English class describing our personal philosophy of life:

**"My philosophy of life is escape… It is my last line of defense in coping with reality for it can most often eradicate problems that would otherwise destroy me. When I achieve escape, I gain entrance into a new and beautiful world, of which I am founder and sole occupant… My family life is intolerable. My parents and I exchange perfunctory amenities and my sister's death would be welcome news. Most of the people I know are threats to my existence… My school is a fascist sewer that continues to pollute and poison itself daily with its own waste… I am basically escaping my own paranoid self. I am attempting to cope with my psychic malfunctioning and my own inner conflicts… Total escape of course is death. It is highly desirable and thoroughly pragmatic when painless, swift and unexpected."**

I was barely 17 when I wrote this. My teacher gave me an A+ and noted in ink, "You are following in the American tradition of escape which Thoreau, Huck Finn and many others have used."

My teacher should have sent me for psychiatric help (or maybe she was crazy too). But to be fair, this was, after all, 1967: She may have thought me just one more mixed-up, angry adolescent caught up in America's every-spreading Counterculture of long hair, Vietnam protests, grass, acid, Haight-Ashberry, Buddha, Free Love and a mind-blowing phalanx of new music, new words, new politics.

To be sure, I was caught up in all this exciting Aquarian-Age stuff, and it was slowly seeping into my confused, angry, sad mixed-state, wearing down my compulsion to get high grades or win debates or worry about college and career. This was the year I promised myself never to grow up into a fat middle-class male with a Stepford wife and 2.5 kids and a toxic job, a nondescript suburban house and two cars and all the other crap my parents and their peers so deeply valued.

Those parents may have been members of what's called "The Greatest Generation." But now they were merely trying to grab their share of what they defined as "The Good Life." And that life wasn't on my flight plan.

This probably held true for millions of other high-school rebels back then. But some of them, like me, didn't know the difference between the galvanic, liberating Counterculture—and insanity.

What also probably held true for millions of rebels my age back then is that, myself included, we quietly kept one proverbial foot in the value-system of our parents. No matter how much dope I smoked, how much acid-rock I nodded out to, no matter all the existentialism and Asian religion I read—I still wanted to go to college and become someone who succeeded at something in America's established society.

Christ, all the way back to when I was 12 in seventh grade, 1962, my parents, relatives, friends' parents, neighbors, teachers and principals told my classmates and me over and over and over that if we didn't get into and graduate from a good university (preferably Ivy League) with at least a Bachelor's degree (preferably more, like an M.D.) and have a good career (lots of status, power and income), we would suffer a life of failure and misery. Hell.

I believed this nonsense. I was terrified of failure on their terms (even though I later spent most of high school and college outwardly trying to reject their terms). I had no way of knowing that the guy who would co-found Microsoft in 1975 and become one of the world's richest men, was a Harvard dropout.

# ROLLING STONED

A few weeks before my junior year ended, Springfield's chapter of the businessmen's group Kiwanis honored two outstanding young men from my class by selecting them to attend a week-long summer program during which model boys from high schools all over New Jersey would create their own model government, and, in theory, learn all sorts of great things about American democracy.

For reasons I understand, Kiwanis chose Bob Ackerman, a star scholar-athlete-nice-handsome-super-straight guy who wanted to attend West Point—and for reasons I'll never understand, they chose me. My whole being wanted to leave, as already arranged, for Nantucket ASAP; I hated the thought of having to delay my departure for a week to participate in what I viewed as some closet-fascist conclave. But I saw no way out at the time, so I angrily packed and my father drove me down to Rutgers University where this idiot shindig would take place.

We get there and walk into a building where a few hundred all-star boys are assembling for some kind of roll call—and this fat man in a paramilitary uniform comes up to us and says to me, "Son, you have to get your hair cut, it's too long."

Too long? My hair barely skirts the top of my ears. Is this guy crazy? Well, this was 1967, the Counterculture still wasn't pandemic, and, believe it or not, long hair on guys was still taboo for a lot of jerks.

I firmly tell the guy I won't cut my hair; the Constitution protects me. He says I'll be thrown out if I don't get it cut immediately. Perhaps this Nazi struck some repressed antiauthority stuff in my father because he backed me up unconditionally. The Nazi held his ground. We marched out, and I was on my way to Nantucket the next day. (I later heard my school principal was furious over my behavior. Fuck him, I thought.)

o o o

Finally, joyously, I was back on Nantucket for my second season at Nobska Playhouse. But please let me digress again: You see, during the months before my return to the island, my high-school buddies and I, like kids nationwide, were smoking a lot of marijuana and having lots of fun. I loved grass because for a few sublime hours my psychological problems—like chronic anxiety, nonstop projection and sharp downward moodswings—disappeared.

And yet even when wiped out on Panama Red, I couldn't shake what had become over time my sadly warped view of girls. Since I first, around age 10 or 11, realized just how extraordinarily different males and females were and concurrently felt my first sexual attraction to girls at school, I loved this mysterious, thrilling other gender. For the first time I cared about how I looked to them; like the other guys my age I carried a comb in my back pocket (which felt pretty cool). Soon I was enjoying—as best I could enjoy anything by then; I was already losing touch with joy—the coed parties kids were throwing, the dancing, the make-out sessions.

But around the time I ran away to Chicago, my self-image took another plunge: While guys my age were pairing off with girls and graduating to advanced sex, I increasingly couldn't see why any pretty, smart, popular girl would ever be attracted to me in any way; I felt acutely unworthy of such girls ever liking me, let alone loving me. And the more attracted I was to them, the more I shied away, turning one after another into an unapproachable goddess.

No wonder why, a few years later, when I wasn't a crazed-libido-self-adoring manic, I much too often, consciously or not, ended up involved with a woman I wasn't physically or emotionally attracted to. Because that's what I deserved.

And when I wasn't pulling this nonsense, I gravitated to asexual friendships with women older than I—my proxy-mothers—with whom I felt safe and happy, perhaps loved, I'm not sure.

o o o

Please forgive the digression. Sometimes I feel as if my mind and my life have always pushed on in a state of digression. (What this means I'm not sure, but it sounds good).

So we're back on Nantucket, summer 1967. (Joel has come with me this time; I'd spent all winter raving about the island to him.) In the course of this summer, I can honestly say I reached and sustained a high, perhaps hypomanic degree of happiness I'd never felt before. I worked and played with more truly good, fun, talented people than I'd ever before met at one time in one place. And the journal I was keeping has many weird, scrawled, two-word entries like "Stoned Again!!!!!"

Yeah we smoked a lot of grass and hashish; more nights than not, after the show, I sat on our stage with the rest of the Nobska cast and crew and we all got wrecked and talked nonsense and laughed hysterically with Sgt. Pepper's blaring over the sound system. In time, as most always with grass, we'd feel terrific hunger (the "munchies") and en masse go to our favorite late-night coffee shop for tuna melts and fries.

I was still neurotic, but I managed to sidetrack my inferiority feelings about girls and have an exciting romantic fling with the kind of bright, foxy blonde I'd normally back away from. Equally important is that my several theater friends became for me a collective antidepressant; they were affectionate with me, never put me down, accepted me without question. I felt loved, especially by the older, pretty actresses whom I asexually adored. No wonder I so remember that summer.

# POW'd

"Here we go, back into hell for another year."

That's what I grumbled to Melissa, one of my classmates, as we entered our high school to begin our senior year.

I'd returned to Springfield from Nantucket a few days earlier, but the elation I'd felt on the island had snapped into sadness and rage alternating with epiphanies and quirky highs: a nascent manic-depressive mixed state. My earlier hatred of my high school had intensified. I saw the place as my prison. Likewise, I saw Springfield as my prison. New Jersey as my prison. My father, most of all, as my prison. He fought to control me, I fought him for my freedom, for my fucking sanity. Our relationship was crystalline: We hated each other.

And thanks to my neurotic, habitual transference (seeing most every adult as my bad or good parent), I also hated all of my school's idiot administrators and those teachers I deemed incompetent or fascist. I denounced them for being totalitarian, malignant and self-insulated from the extraordinary social change going on just beyond the broad, well-tended lawns of our huge, arrogant Colonial-Revival building.

Years later, a good shrink told me that sadness always lies beneath anger. She also advised me that what we hate in others is what we hate in ourselves.

Looking back, therefore, I was very sad that senior year, and didn't know it. In addition, I didn't realize I had zero self-esteem, didn't know this led to self-hate. No, I was too busy hating the world.

And I meanwhile spent most of that last year doing only enough classwork to get by and virtually no extracurricular stuff. Instead, when not in school, I spent a lot of time alone in my room reading all sorts of books and magazines that had nothing to do with school.

Those many hours alone in my room were among the only waking periods when I felt anything near to mental peace. This peace I also felt, and often with tremendous freedom and exhilaration, during my countless, solitary trips to plays, museums and galleries in Manhattan, during my solitary walks through a densely forested park near my house, during my poetry writing and always during my halcyon memories of Nantucket. I was drifting away from the few people I called friends, even away from Joel. When not stoned, my stress-pain level with people was abnormally high. I was becoming a loner. A loner who could not fully see how badly he wanted to love and be loved. You don't have to be manic-depressive to end up this way, but the undertow of that madness helped drown my attempts to connect, on a deep and lasting level, with other human beings.

These attempts especially encompassed my friends. Despite my growing loner behavior, I forever imagined and worried about what they were thinking about me when I was with them and saying about me when I wasn't. I called this neurotic anxiety PSPT (people-say-people-think); I didn't know at the time that I was immersed in paranoid projection. Manic-depressives like me, when not lucky enough to have a good shrink and good meds, believe they are the center of the universe.

Nevertheless, when not alone in my room reading, I tried to do things with my friends, like listening to the newest rock groups, moviegoing, theater going; talking about books, politics, philosophy;

reading each other's poetry; old-fashioned gossip. We loved to hang out at Swingles, on U.S. Route 22 in Springfield, our favorite truck-stop diner. We loved smoking grass and dropping speed (various kinds of amphetamine)—some of us were into crystal Methedrine, the speed of all speed.

That I did a lot of amphetamines doesn't surprise me. I loved the 12-hour flight-to-the-moon high of extraordinary energy and euphoria. I didn't like the inevitable "crash" (coming down off the drug was akin to a long, bad hangover), but I put up with it, eased it with grass.

Only recently did I realize the high of speed mimicked clinical mania, and the crash mimicked clinical depression. Meaning I unwittingly enjoyed making myself mentally ill. And when I wasn't somewhere along the spectrum of speed or grass, I defaulted to my daily, sober, tortured thinking and behavior.

Either way, I was angrier than ever at my parents and school—and at America, which like me in 1968 was going mad: The King and Kennedy murders, race riots, Vietnam, napalmed babies, protests galore, police brutality: These and other symptoms of a national descent into malice and psychosis only worsened my already black, angry moods, which in turn powered my not caring about high school or about getting into a good college.

Example: I'd hated math for years but was taking and loathing an extra algebra course because I mistakenly thought I needed it for college. Bouncing around my mixed-state at the time, I, the once-stellar student, decided to eject algebra from my life. I stopped doing the homework and I sat in the back of the class ignoring the teacher and reading news magazines or novels. The teacher eventually warned me that if I kept up my bad behavior, she'd have to fail me for the year. I clearly remember my telling her, "You have no choice but to fail me." Come June, she did. And I didn't give a fuck.

Besides, despite my failing algebra, I only dropped from grade-rank number six in my graduating class to number seven. When I heard this, I didn't care; I was too busy scoring Dexedrine from a 14-year-old girl dealer who routinely robbed it from her father-doctor's office.

This was, nonetheless, college application time. The only school I wanted to go to was Antioch College in Yellow Springs, Ohio. I'd often heard about Antioch and after some research decided its unconventional curricula made it the perfect place for an anti-establishment kid like me. My father hated the idea of my attending Antioch. He'd abruptly decided I was no longer his rotten son; now, once more, I was his trophy son. And despite my falling grades and Dumpster SAT scores and total withdrawal from extracurricular activities—the asshole coerced me into applying to the Ivy League's Harvard, Columbia and the University of Pennsylvania. He also assured my rejection from Antioch by refusing to fund my flying to Yellow Springs for an interview (the only way I could explain and counter my anemic academics and test scores).

He refused to see that I wasn't exactly Ivy League material. He refused to hear me when I yelled I didn't want to go to those fucking schools and even if I wanted to I couldn't possibly get in.

I was right on all counts. On April 15, Antioch, and the Ivies, rejected me. Luckily, Joel had earlier encouraged me to apply to a "safety school," one certain to take me. So I applied to NYU (New York University), a non-Ivy, traditional and very expensive private institution in Manhattan's Greenwich Village.

NYU took me. Whoopee! I didn't care.

The real joke is that a month later, probably because of my earlier pubic-speaking success, I was picked as one of three students to write and deliver a speech to my class during our graduation ceremony. Graduation night, I opened my speech by noting that two weeks earlier

Robert Kennedy lay dying on the floor of a hotel in Los Angeles; at the end, I echoed my favorite existential philosopher Jean-Paul Sartre, telling my classmates they had to "create their own meaning and purpose in life" and urging them to develop a "social conscience." An unknown number of the cap-and-gowned kids I addressed were stoned on grass; I think one of my friends was tripping on acid.

Sidebar: I believe I was the only kid in my graduating class who, due to my hating our high school, didn't buy the traditional yearbook. I was also one of the few kids who didn't attend the junior prom or the senior ball—I was making an anger statement, don't know about the others.

# LIBIDOLAND

I'll briefly stop here to note my sexual coming of age was, based on all my reading and conversation, no different than a billion other 11-year-old boys who happened be on Earth when circa 1961 an older buddy of mine turned me on to what he called "jerking-off," that is, masturbation.

Right from the get-go, I loved jerking-off. I did it whenever I could (always instinctively careful to avoid getting caught by my parents)—I did it at night in bed looking at pictures of naked women, in the shower, in my uncle's pool, at summer camp (every camper I knew covertly jerked-off almost nightly) and even while dressing for my bar mitzvah. I also read all the medical stuff I could about sex and rapidly graduated to splendid fantasies about me doing the real thing with a real girl.

All that was pretty normal. The only slight difference is that manic-depressives like me when high and unmedicated are known for having a turbocharged libido. During such periods, I was sex-crazed. I made it with absolutely any woman who wanted me. This could be called "disordered, promiscuous behavior," but I've sure known over the past 40-odd years plenty of non-manic, stable guys, both straight and gay, who fucked-around as much as I; likewise numerous straight and lesbian women I've known. After all, my generation got into heavy sex at the height of the late '60s "Free Love" movement, which was Counterculture code for sleeping around as much as you could.

Anyway, what's really funny here is that the only thing my control-freak father ever said to me about sex, this is true, was when I was 13 and about to leave for summer camp: "Eric, do you know what the word 'masturbation' means?" I nod, yes. "Well, son, some of the boys at camp may masturbate. Don't do it. It's not good for you."

I said nothing. I'd already been jerking-off and enjoying it immensely for the past two years.

In any case, my sex life overall, though reasonably rich, has thus far been routine, nothing really special, and so in this book I don't much talk about it.

# THE SHOW DIDN'T GO ON

After my 1968 high-school graduation, I joyously returned to Nantucket to work at the Nobska Playhouse.

Joel came with me again, working for an electrician during the day and at night helping me do the lights for Nobska's productions.

We had a new cast and crew, good, talented people, though we weren't as tight as the previous summer's group. Not as much dope, not as much zaniness; I didn't care, I was once more on my beloved island.

Joel and I rented a big furnished room in an archetypal Nantucket home a short walk from the heart of town. We usually breakfasted at a colorful diner favored by the island's natives. And after the Nobska show, we'd often sit at a little table in our room and have good talks while sipping Chianti and munching on fresh thick bread or Ritz crackers dipped in some kind of cheese sauce. Those late nights at the table are still among my warmest memories. My interpersonal stress level with Joel through our years of friendship was as close to zero as I could get with another human being.

As in past summers on the island I was once more in a state of mild elation. But halfway through this one my mental state and feelings changed terribly when another friend of mine working at the theater, a more distant and clearly troubled friend, turned me into his enemy. His name was Nathan. Roughly my age, he was the damaged product of a rich family occupying an upper Fifth Avenue co-op in Manhattan. He was semi-estranged from his parents, who, I believe, nonetheless paid for his apartment in an elite neighborhood near the United Nations.

I'd met Nathan on Nantucket at some point during, I think, my first summer there. Either way, I often spent time with him in Manhattan and we smoked his home-grown dope and had a lot of fun together.

Only later did I learn Nathan had a serious psychiatric history and had been hospitalized at least once. And I much later was told Nathan was either gay, in the closet, or confused.

Okay. So we're back in my Nantucket summer of 1968, and Nathan, like an enraged jealous lover, suddenly becomes madly possessive of me. He resents my spending time with any other person, especially women. Then he abruptly stops talking to me except to insult me. I honestly don't know what I'd done to win this baffling, painful and depressing treatment from a guy who once told me I was the only friend he had.

In short: I was miserable. I let Nathan destroy my summer.

o o o

I thought Nathan was history when I started NYU but then I started receiving remorseful letters and notes from him at my Manhattan dormitory. They said shit like "I'm sorry, I want to see you." I never responded, but he did this for months (I didn't know about stalkers back then) until finally giving up. No fucking way did I ever want to see him again.

By the end of that summer, moreover, my fury at Nathan had generalized to all people. I'd decided Sartre was right, "Hell is other people." Nathan was hell.

Anyone I'd meet at NYU would be hell, and thus I vowed to meet no one, to have no friends at school, no friends at all, except Joel, who was in college a thousand miles away.

# RUN SILENT RUN DEEPER

I was 18 at the start of my freshman year at NYU, and I was tumbling into what would become a seven-month-long, clinical depression. I had never before sunk so far for so long with such pain.

I knew how lousy I felt but at the time didn't know what to call it. Over and over, I tried to describe my feelings orally and in writing. Here's one attempt, a prose poem I wrote only six weeks into my first semester while sitting against a tree:

**A Few Minutes in Washington Square Park—An October Afternoon**

**A couple is necking on the grass. He is on top of her, and she taps the back of his neck. Their lips part in two smiles, two laughs, and then once more a kiss. I once did the same.**

**Two little boys are playing football. They debate, "Tackle or touch?" I, too, once did the same.**

**But now bored and afraid, I do nothing. I am dull. I thought I'd love college—its courses, its work, its INTELLECTUAL stimulation. But I can't get involved or concerned over anything. Energy is gone. And so is motivation—desire. Nothing seems to have any meaning or relevance.**

**I daydream through French and wonder how I'll ever make it through the year: The age of self-sacrifice is over.**

**It's autumn—finally—and this afternoon is so alive, yet so quiet. The art students are sitting on the grass. Do they enjoy what they are doing? Are they interested? I walked through the library before and saw people going about their research. It no longer interests me.**

**I only note the quiet, breathing motion about me. The flow of humans and pigeons and footballs. The two little boys are still throwing their football. Each pass sends the ball into the dirt and dead leaves—their stadium.**

**There seems to be a spirit—life itself—all about me. But I cannot indulge; I can't even feel its fringe as it flows past and leaves me to my emptiness.**

**Eric Krueger**
**10/23/68**
**New York City**

These and similar words sum up my start at NYU. I sank deeper with each month, by early February into despair, terror, crying and semi-dysfunction.

And yet by late February, as pilots say, I pulled up—without a psychiatrist or medication; I did so because my miswired brain had finally on its own decided the time had come for me to slowly spiral up into clinical mania.

o o o

In the course of this freshman year, I learned how to play incredibly well what a shrink years later explained to me was a psychological game called "Rescue." I mention it here because, knowingly or not, I continually lapsed into it from circa 1967 to 2006. In my opinion, it is a vicious, psycho-motherfucker rooted in sick self-obsession, love-hunger and paranoia. With it, I have hurt countless people, most of all myself.

You may have played it. You may be playing it now.

Here's how the game works: You play the "Victim." Your "Persecutors"can be your father, ex-lover, professor, employer, DNA, shrink, the universe, or any combination thereof, and more, name them.

I, in turn, play your "Rescuer." My job, via passive and supportive listening and other behaviors, is to help you fight your psychological pain and related tsuris. I always take your side against your persecutors. I sometimes suggest remedial actions you can take; these you consistently sweep aside with a sentence most always beginning with, "Yes, but…"

Once in a rare while, I will ask for your help regarding some difficulty I'm facing, and you will gladly give it out of gratitude—and then snap right back into your victim role. We keep playing—at your home, mine, restaurants, bars, in the car, on the beach, everywhere, always. This can last one night, a few months, or a year, even longer.

Ah, ha. Sooner or later, however, I stop listening to you. I am there physically, but I am light years away and waiting for you to shut up so I can go home and rest until we start up again. But then, sooner or later, I can no longer stand to be your rescuer—I'm thinking fuck you and all your sick, stupid, never-ending existential pain—and I consciously or not do or say something to make you furious with me, to make you feel I've betrayed you and what you think has been our great relationship all along.

So guess what? Now you, still the victim, of course, see me as one of your persecutors. And some poor slob who does or doesn't know better ends up your new rescuer.

Some people live their whole lives as victims. My own trick when clinically depressed is to persuade a rescuer that I am both the victim and my own worst persecutor.

o o o

I promise: this "rescue" stuff was my last topical digression; from here on, I'll try to stay on track.

o o o

Okay, so we're back in late February 1969 and I'm coming out of a vertical dive, heading slowly and at first imperceptibly toward mania.

Part of what boosted me was the intensity and wealth of my second semester's workload. And yes, I broke my no-friends vow and with Ellie, a woman friend from high school attending another college in the city, every other Friday spent an evening of drinking, talking and laughing in a posh Upper East Side bar. Unlike the members of generations before me, I had skipped alcohol in high school in favor of dope. But now, I discovered, after two or three strong Manhattans, my demons disappeared, at least for a few hours.

I meantime met another woman, Harriet, who sat next to me in two courses. For reasons I'll never know and don't care to sort out, Harriet, some 10 years older than I, a painter and an uncommonly beautiful woman, was attracted to me, or pitied me or whatever. I didn't want a romantic relationship of any kind with anyone, but with her I snapped right into a perfect rescue game lasting the entire academic year. Since we started the game while I was still clinically depressed, I naturally played the utterly miserable victim—of myself, NYU, life, the cosmos. She played the loving rescuer. I'm not sure we ever realized how hard we were playing, I do know I was happily addicted to it.

I gained still more illusory yardage by spending every other weekend at home in Springfield, only 45 minutes by bus from Manhattan. Getting away from my music-blaring acid-head roommates and from the city, which I'd once so loved and now so hated as "antihuman," clearly helped me. Growing evermore compulsive about my academic performance, I spent almost every waking hour of those weekends doing required reading and term papers. My parents didn't hassle me at all, which also helped.

Thanks to these home visits and to Ellie, Harriet and my dynamite, junior-and senior-level courses in modern European history, dramatic literature, history of architecture and geology (where the professor, 30 years before Al Gore, passionately warned us about human-induced global climate change) —and thanks to all of these factors fueling and fueled by the shift in the electrochemistry of my brain, my spirits rose higher every day. I even made time to smoke dope with my roommates while we played Monopoly, which left me laughing for the first time in months.

Through the spring of 1969, I kept up my mad, academic overworking—and liked it. I worked so hard at first because I was honestly scared to death of failing all my courses; but in time, I told myself and others that I wanted peak grades to make sure I'd get into Livingston College, a brand new, experimental, politically left-liberal division of Rutgers University, which I'd applied to in February. But to be honest, I didn't quite know why I was driving myself so insanely hard.

I ended the school year with an A in every course except French, a required course I hated and did minimal work for. A few weeks before finishing my freshman year, I dropped mescaline twice and decided I would reward myself for my sterling academic performance by vacationing in the Cayman Islands. I was happy. Too happy. Livingston accepted me. I got happier still.

## *"You Say You Want a Revolution..."*

The Beatles, 1968.

I was bouncing from hypomania to mania and back by May 1969. For starters, I joined SDS (Students for a Democratic Society), back then a famous national organization of liberal and left-wing student radicals which in time mutated into a small gang of closet-Stalinists who self-annihilated.

I joined SDS because a mesmeric leftist history professor and some fascinating books about neocapitalism and imperialism had convinced me we had to have a socialist revolution in America. Or so I told myself. In reality I joined SDS primarily to be cool, to latch onto an identity as a fearless radical quoting Marxist historians at length to anyone who'd listen. Of course, the more manic I became that summer, the more extreme, the more insane my politics.

To enhance my new persona, I wore dark, "tear-drop" aviator glasses because I'd seen a lot of SDS alpha-types wearing them. Those guys looked tough; I wanted to be tough, as in my early teens when I wanted to be James Bond.

Only this was much better than Bond because the political activities I took part in—demonstrating, screaming slogans, confronting pigs (police officers and anyone else we deemed worthy of death), taking over campus buildings, marching onto U.S military bases, getting clubbed and gassed and arrested—I saw as brave, ultra-cool and history-making. And for me thus masked and made up for my essential feelings of weakness, of being no one and nothing.

What I didn't realize until years later is that I, and perhaps countless other college "radicals," weren't as radical as we liked to think. Indeed, like my rebel friends and I in high school, we were covertly careful to keep one foot in the Revolution and the other in American middle-class convention. No activist I went to college with dropped out to join a commune in the desert or an underground political cell. None of us let go of the white suburban culture we'd come from and had internalized. Talk about schizoid.

Here's the kicker: I attended in June 1969 with some radical friends the national SDS convention in Chicago. This was the event where SDS leaders Mark Rudd and Bernadine Dohrn and their buddies decided in front of the convention to essentially disband SDS and proclaim the ascendance of a new far more revolutionary organization they dubbed "Weatherman."

A night or two after Weatherman's coup d'état, I somehow ended up sitting on the floor in a meeting in some Chicago apartment with a bunch of other radicals. Rudd and Dohrn were leading the meeting, better still, holding court. Rudd was talking and at some point said something really insane about how we were going to mount a violent revolution against the U.S. government. I interrupted him, politely objecting to his psychotic goal by saying we didn't have the "mass base" a successful popular uprising requires.

This sick, spoiled kid born in Irvington, N.J, not far from Springfield, this egomaniacal radical who'd recently won national press coverage by leading a student revolt at Columbia University, simply stares at me at me and sternly, dismissively says, I'll never forget it, "You are an objective agent of the bourgeoisie."

I reverted to being a scared child and said nothing more. I felt as if God had just denounced me.

In a car the next morning heading home, one of the passengers with me, a leftist history professor to whom I mentioned Rudd's accusation, looked grimly at me and quietly said, "The first person to call a political opponent an 'objective agent of the bourgeoisie'—was Stalin."

Self-styled Stalin Mark Rudd, after running from the law for seven years, finally gave up on his revolution and in 1978 surrendered to authorities (he was fined and put on probation).

I temporarily abandoned the revolution and, inching up toward mania, turned to other odd exploits.

o o o

That same summer of 1969, I read Thomas Wolfe's famous novel, *Look Homeward, Angel*, set in a fictional town based on the real city of Asheville, North Carolina, where Wolfe had grown up. I loved this book. A little too much.

With money from where I don't know, I flew from New Jersey to Asheville, got a hotel room and stayed for a week. I visited the Wolfe home and other Wolfe locations. I also checked out Asheville's bars, stores and diners—and in the course of this met a few dope-smoking kids who instantly befriended me, amazed I'd come to their town all the way from New Jersey "jus' 'cause you read a book?"

And then from Asheville in rapid sequence, by train (because Wolfe seemed to love trains) to see friends in D.C.; and then driving up to Ithaca, N.Y. with my longtime buddy Russell who was soon to start his second year at Cornell; followed by a weekend with a close older friend attending Douglass College (the elite women's division of Rutgers) and a week or so with Harriet at her farm in upstate New York, and so on.

Manics, in my experience anyway, love to keep moving. Depressives love sitting alone in a room and staring at nothing; most of all, they love sleeping and sometimes wish they could sleep forever and sometimes make that happen.

Okay, so Livingston finally opened, and to further my desire to be cool and tough, I bought a Triumph Trophy 250 motorcycle. Bikes were vogue then (or so I thought) and Triumphs were status machines (or so I thought). Mine would not only enhance my persona but also help me move very fast anywhere anytime, and this, of course, I loved.

# HANDCUFFED TO THE BOTTOM OF AN ABANDONED MINESHAFT

I considered Livingston College of Rutgers University my dream school. It was only a few miles from the main Rutgers campus in New Brunswick, N.J., but at the time it was markedly different from the rest of the university and most other schools. We had no required courses, no traditional grading system (merely pass-fail-honors), an impressive, left-liberal faculty with superb academic credentials, and, most notably, Livingston was committed to fighting the socioeconomic inequality in America that had ultimately sparked the race riots of the '60s.

o o o

I was pretty manic by the time my first year at Livingston started, a prime benchmark of this being Professor Altman's creative writing class. The first day it met, Altman told us our first assignment would be to write our autobiographies.

I snapped into manic transference, seeing him as my controlling father, as an authoritarian violating student rights as defined by Livingston's mission statement (actually, as defined by me). In turn, I barked at him in front of some 25 other students that I didn't come to Livingston to be told what to write—I was going to write whatever I wanted.

I don't recall his reaction. But I clearly remember standing up and storming out of the classroom. Once outside, I looked behind me—and there were all the other students. A short time later, Livingston allowed us to set up our own independent writing course, which a well-known Rutgers literary critic and stellar English professor helped us with.

My accidentally destroying Altman's course elated me; but I was soon bouncing around in an increasingly fierce mixed state, which led me to pull out of a radical, left-wing political group I'd helped launch, cut most of my classes, withdraw from my friends, and, unknowingly but desperately, try to escape from a lover, a bright, foxy, loving woman, for whom my growing problems no longer had room.

Much like that NYU autumn a year earlier, I was spiraling down into the horror house of clinical depression. However this was worse than NYU—it was, to paraphrase someone else, Katrina in slow-motion, at once breaching, flattening and flooding both myself and those who cared about me.

When friends on campus asked me how I was doing, I tried to describe my indescribable pain and then lapsed into crying.

When I tried and failed to study or write, I cried. And yet I didn't know what at root I was so sad about, only that it was something vague and terrible.

I tried to recapture happiness by going home, an hour away, on weekends; this attempt to recreate my previous spring at NYU failed, as did my ability to concentrate on anything academic. I was a mess.

So much so that once while home I overnight broke out into body-wide hives. Our pharmacy supplied us with some kind of lotion my father (not I, which is curious, since I wasn't an infant, I was 19) rubbed all over me. Next day the hives were gone: a perfect psychogenic disorder, their cause not physical, but rather my super-stressed-out mind.

o o o

During this depression, I was seeing the school psychologist, Marshall, at first once weekly but in time every day. I cried a lot in front of him, cried over my mangled feelings and behavior. All he did, every session, was to tell me to "get in touch" with my feelings.

Get in touch? I'm sitting there telling him how much I hate myself and crying so badly my vision is blurred and he doesn't think I'm in touch?

His approach confused and pained me. Here's the worst part: At times, when I was talking and sobbing, he'd turn away from me in his big swivel chair and gaze out the window.

After seven months of the window stunt and hearing me cry over my life, after never diagnosing me with clinical depression, never referring me to a psychiatrist for antidepressant medication (treatment I didn't know about then)—Marshall decides I should spend a few days in the Rutgers infirmary, or better still, leave Livingston indefinitely. I break down and beg him to let me stay. He agrees. But the next day I cry to a woman friend, Paula (yet another in a long series of rescuers that year) that I want to die, or perhaps that I was determined to kill myself, I forget which.

Either way, she got scared and notified Marshall, who summoned my parents to campus. The rest is dark and hazy. I only remember my father asking some friends of mine to take me with them to a movie they were going to that night. They did.

The movie didn't help. And all their subsequent efforts to help me failed. They didn't understand how bad off I was. How could they? I didn't understand. The goddamned school shrink didn't understand.

o o o

During this depression I was still writing, or trying to write, in the journal I'd begun on Nantucket three years earlier. Here are some telling quotes:

**—March 22, 1970**

**I sit at my desk and pick at the dirt under my nails—now that I'm alone. I fight with the urge to pull at my hair, for this symptom returns as soon as I try to work on my paper on *Othello*, a play for which I've given the worst reading, possibly, of my life. And as I write this, I pick at my nose, scratch my face and think about how I haven't been out all day, how I constantly stuff food—fattening food—into myself and how vegetative I am. I no longer feel human.**

**—April 14, 1970**

**I am so anal-retentive at present. Everything, thought, feelings, fears, all bottled up, corked up inside me. No one can help me and I can't help myself.**

**—April 20, 1970**

**I woke up depressed. The situation is very critical, though I'm exhausted at the moment. At this point I can't write about 'it.' If I could kill myself... I was almost hysterical a few hours ago. I really cracked up today. Will I have to leave school?**

**—May 1, 1970**

**I have less and less control over my behavior. I see people at the library, taking notes, reading and writing; I want to be one of them but I'm not. I'm nothing at this point. You wouldn't believe me. It's evermore harder to face myself. Oh shit.**

**—June 3, 1970**

**I really get upset every time I think of the past year, of what lies ahead of me, for all seems to have gone wrong, all seems a failure while I do nothing to remedy things. The same story: no energy, no faith in myself, no hope. When I think of what other kids my age are doing at this moment, I stop thinking.**

I froze into near-total dysfunction. Marshall still wanted me to leave school, but for me leaving meant abject failure. Absolute disgrace. I was still half-consciously hoping I would spiral back up, but it didn't happen. Instead, I was too paralyzed to even pick my courses for the coming year, so Marshall helped me; at one point, looking over the course offerings, he said, "There's a new course here, a movie course, it's about film history and criticism, it could be fun."

That was the only smart thing Marshall ever said to me. I'd never heard of film studies, but I agreed.

o o o

About this time, Nixon's invasion of Cambodia spurred most every college in the country to shut down in protest (remember Kent State?). Livingston shut down, its kids joining armies of other kids in a march on Washington. I stayed at Livingston, the campus was empty, and I sat in the library each day trying and failing to read books and magazines, skimming newspaper reports about protests nationwide, wondering how my sophomore year would end.

I found out how after Livingston formally announced that grades for the second semester would be based on our work prior to the school's closing.

I went home.

I felt saved.

# ON THE ROAD OFF THE MAP

Still morbidly depressed, I got a summer job with a moving company. I was a "packer." My partner and I would drive to someone's home in a small van and carefully wrap all the small household goods, put the stuff in big cardboard boxes and take it to our main office (next day the furniture-and-appliance guys would show up in an 18-wheeler and do their heavy-lifting thing).

Packing was easy, and I began to enjoy our driving all over parts of New Jersey I'd never seen before. My partner at the wheel, I was the navigator, holding maps on my lap and calling out directions to this home or that. My ongoing anxiety and despair notwithstanding, I ever-so-slowly, out of my awareness, drifted up out of depression and into a mixed state.

At least once weekly, we had to drive past Newark Airport to hit the New Jersey Turnpike. Every time we approached the Turnpike entrance, I saw with growing fascination small groups of hitchhikers—most in faded jeans and tie-dyed shirts, most with backpacks and sleeping bags, and some with handmade signs saying "Chicago" or "San Francisco."

While looking at these peoples one day, I realized I could do the same thing.

Here is my journal entry for Sunday, July 19, 1970:

**In the three blurred weeks since my last entry, I continued working… After saving over five-hundred dollars, I've decided to hitch across the country; I'm leaving tomorrow. The trip is my last hope vis a vis losing weight, recharging the excitatory tissues of my brain, and having a good summer. I don't know what will happen out on the road, and I've already had a good many paranoid fantasies; I however do know I've got to leave, get out of here, and salvage myself in the next seven weeks, for I'm not much better now than I was a month or two months ago. And so, excited and fearful and subdued about the trip, I prepare for departure. See you in seven weeks. Maybe.**

With a well-stocked backpack, sleeping bag and canteen, I next morning walked from my home to U.S. Route 22 west, stuck out my thumb, caught my first ride in minutes.

My subsequent rides—I logged 18 long ones in three and a half days—got me to San Francisco, the only destination I had in mind.

I was lucky: Hitching was safe that summer of 1970 and hitchhikers were all over the roads; a lot of friendly drivers with a lot of miles to cover were out there too. Plus, I was alone (drivers were more likely to stop for one person), I looked boyish and innocent, I was wearing a nice collared shirt, and with the people who gave me rides, I was always, always polite, the pleasing-child me.

Not surprisingly, in retrospect, the wild adventure of getting to San Francisco and the city's hypnotic beauty ended my mixed-state. Mania, so stealthy, was on the move, like Viet Cong slipping through the jungle.

Why I don't recall but I next hitched 500 miles down the magnificent California coast to Los Angeles. Thanks to some distant relatives, who let me crash at their L.A. house, I spent five days hitching with ease all over the city—more than one driver offered me a lit joint—met a lot of good people and loved the place, loved the stuff I'd never seen before like Spanish architecture, wooded canyons, freeways to everywhere, and, of course, Disneyland. Most of all, I fell in love with L.A.'s infinite offering of space and light.

By now I was edging into hypomania, although I simply thought I'd finally kicked depression and was actually happy again. So happy I wanted to keep moving, and moving. From L.A. I hitched to San Diego and from there to the Grand Canyon and then Vegas and then north to Yosemite and northward still to Portland and Seattle and then east to Spokane and down through Idaho and up into Montana and South Dakota and then down through Yellowstone, the Grand Tetons, the Rockies, Boulder and back up to Omaha and then Des Moines where I grabbed Interstate 80 and rides that took me deep into Pennsylvania, where I picked up Route 22 east and shot right to Springfield, leaving my last ride less than a mile from my home.

o o o

My timeless, kaleidoscopic, sensory-gala road trip pushed me right through hypomania into borderline clinical mania. What I wrote in my journal in no way conveys the elation and radiant energy I came home with, but I think it's worth a look:

**Thursday, September 3, 1970**

**This will be my last entry for a long time… in fact, this might be the last entry of my journal.**

**I returned from my ten-thousand-mile hitchhiking tour of the country two days ago. The trip lasted six weeks—and it did more for my head than all my months of psychotherapy.**

**I've somehow managed to revive my interest in life, thanks to the trip; and I've also gained back some confidence. If this coming year bums out, I'll just pack my knapsack, cut my hair, and move to Boulder, or Bozeman, or Flagstaff, or…**

**Yes, I feel much better. And for better or worse, I just don't feel like writing in the journal anymore. I felt so free on the trip because I made the wise decision not to try and force myself to take notes or to keep a journal; as Marshall says, my writing in it tends to divorce me from my feelings; and life is all about feelings.**

**So this is it. I'll be at school in a week or so. I drove down today and had a great, two-hour rap with Marshall; from now on, I'll only be going to him when I feel like it. In the meantime, I'm just relaxing with music and dope. Whatever happens, happens.**

# SOARING ON EMPTY

Back at Livingston, I shot off the launch pad into clinical mania.

Higher than ever before, I did odd things. Like deciding I was a great photographer and buying a Nikon camera to take pictures of street signs. Like hitching into Manhattan, an hour from Livingston, to photograph whatever I deemed visually significant. And since my trip out West had taught me I could hitch almost anywhere, at least back then, I hitched up to Boston and dropped in on people I knew from high school; from there I hitched down to Washington, D.C. so I could drop in on friends from my Nantucket days.

When I pit-stopped back at Livingston, I ignored my courses, already in progress, and got very weird. For instance, I borrowed my friend Melinda's car ostensibly for a quick errand—and disappeared with it. First to a local liquor store, where the owner refused to sell me a six-pack because my driver's license clearly showed me underage. I didn't care, I wanted the damn beer from this Nazi-father-figure so I started a fistfight with him. Someone broke it up. Next day at dawn, I threw a brick at the liquor store's big front window and shattered it. Then I jumped into Melinda's car and drove into Manhattan, weaving through the heavy traffic and thinking I was racing in the Daytona 500.

Early that evening, I drove over to the Upper East Side, got picked up by a rich private-boarding-school girl and spent the night with her in some ritzy hotel. I'm blank after that, save that I drove back to Livingston and returned to a much-relieved Melinda her car. After which I went to the shop where the year before I'd bought my Triumph Trophy 250 (which I sold during my prior depression) and this time, with a rubber check (the dealer trusted me), upgraded to a bigger, more powerful Triumph 650—and drove it back to Manhattan, where I did strange things like driving the bike in the rain on the sidewalks of JFK international airport at 4 a.m. until some cops told me to cut it out.

I was back at Livingston when my motorcycle check bounced and the dealer asked me to return the Triumph 650, which I did—I wanted to show him I wasn't a thief. I wanted to show him how terrific I was. In fact, I thought everything I did was fabulous.

On CNN recently, I heard a shrink say that psychopaths know the difference between right and wrong—and don't care, go right ahead and do whatever they want. For schizophrenics, on the other hand, right and wrong don't exist.

Thus, I was moving at this point into what's called schizoaffective disorder—a mean brew of manic-depression and schizophrenia.

Oh well, back on campus, I met and quickly declared my love to a freshman woman who didn't quite know what to do with me and soon realized I was crazy. She told me she already had a boyfriend, a junior at the University of Rochester in upstate New York. In fact, she said, she was going to fly up there that night to spend the weekend with him.

I followed her to the airport, where I bounced a check and flew after her to Rochester. At the university, I found the dorm room of a cousin of mine who was a student there and, though baffled by my sudden appearance, let me stay with him. Around 2 a.m., maniacally unable to sleep and bored, I went down to the dorm's security office, stole an officer's shirt from a laundry basket, put it on, started walking around—and got arrested by campus cops who turned me over to the Rochester police; they booked me on charges of criminal trespass and petty larceny.

I loved all this. The handcuffs, mug shot, fingerprinting. And yet once in a cell alone, I got hold of a big plastic bag and put it over my head to stop breathing. A guard saw this and ripped the bag off my head.

My next stop a day later was Rochester's Monroe County Penitentiary. I thought it was neat, like Disneyland with lots of cool black guys who thought I was whacked-out and left me alone.

I was released from the pen after a week or so because the judge who arraigned me, after listening to me babble about defending myself and shouting a lot, and in agreement with my public defender who told me I was crazy—committed me to the Monroe Community Hospital's psychiatric ward.

Remember, through all of this, I honestly believed I was normal. Problem was these people didn't understand.

Although I enjoyed the psych ward at first, I soon wanted out badly, wanted to get moving fast again; I insisted to the shrink in charge that I was sane but she said I had to stay. I was allowed to phone Russell, who at some point drove up from Cornell to see me. I told him I was fine and didn't understand why they wouldn't let me go. Russell quietly said, "I talked with your shrink. She thinks you're crazy."

He didn't say what he thought. Looking back, I sometimes suspect Russell and some other people I would meet over the years got a vicarious charge out of my actually behaving in ways they didn't dare. I lived their fantasies, went mad on their behalf.

Whatever Russell's opinion of me, he called my father and told him what was going on. The next day my father and his brother, my attorney-uncle Jerry, flew up to Rochester; and Jerry, always the fixer, got my judge to free me on the condition that I immediately go back to New Jersey and get psychiatric treatment.

I did see a psychiatrist, but only once, and without consulting anyone went back to Livingston, where a few manic days later I accepted an invitation from Morgan, our dean of students and a psychoanalyst—who knew and liked me from campus politics the year before—to talk with him in his office.

When I got there he spoke softly, kindly, "Eric, we both know you're not well. You're at the point where no one here can help you. You've got be hospitalized for a while."

I tried to pretend I agreed with him, pretend I knew I was crazy and needed expert care. Perhaps part of me really did agree with him.

Whatever the case, Morgan recommended three renowned, private, expensive mental hospitals. I chose Carrier Clinic, about an hour from Rutgers in rural-rich-horse-country Belle Mead, N.J. I knew a little about Carrier because of my mother's treatment there. I viewed it as a resort, I thought it would make for a great vacation; in fact, I thought I'd be living in Disneyland.

My father drove me out to Belle Mead. I remember that October night, it was a dazzling, angry tapestry of blacks, reds and purples, and I was shouting at my father, who said nothing, kept driving.

# THEY MADE IT OFFICIAL

Carrier doesn't want to admit me at first. They think, I later learn, I am too violent. Admittedly, I am pacing all over and shouting in the plush waiting area, and banging things.

A shrink interviews me and afterward tells me for one reason or another I'll have to wait a while to be admitted. Full-blown manics like me hate to wait for anything, they freak-out when a person or event interrupts their pressured movement through time and space. So I shout at the shrink, "I'm sick of waiting! Life is just waiting to die!"

He ignores this comment and has an orderly take me back to the waiting area, where, so eager to be admitted, I calm myself down; and when a nurse brings me a tray of milk and cookies, I thank her as politely and sanely as I can.

I'm finally admitted and taken to Edwards Hall. This is a locked ward for newcomers. No one in, no one out, unless a nurse sitting behind what looks like bullet-proof glass presses a button which sounds a loud buzzer and briefly unlocks a door only big enough for one person to pass into or out of the rest of the large facility.

Edwards itself is a row of nicely spaced rooms, comfortably and tastefully furnished, and painted in calming earth tones, each with an equally calming view of the calming wooded hospital grounds, each with its own complete bathroom, each with a lock-less door opening onto a central earth-toned corridor.

CC-9

# COUNTY COURT OF THE COUNTY OF UNION

In the matter of the Application
for your commitment
to the Carr ier Clinic, Belle Mead, N.J.

NOTICE OF HEARING

RECEIVED
NOV 13 1970
CARRIER CLINIC
MEDICAL RECORDS

TO Eric Krueger

WHEREAS, application having been made for your commitment to the Carrier Clinic, Belle Mead, New Jersey

YOU ARE HEREBY NOTIFIED that a hearing with regard thereto will be held on the 20 th. day of November 19 70 at 10:00 a.m. in the forenoon, at Court House, Elizabeth, New Jersey
If you desire to oppose said application for your commitment to said hospital or any other hospital, you may appear personally or by Counsel at said time and place.

Dated: November 12th 19 70.

Donald Myers
County Adjuster of Union County

jl

STATE OF NEW JERSEY
COUNTY OF ......................

...................... of full age, being duly sworn upon his oath according to law, deposes and says that he served a copy of the notice appearing above, upon the alleged mentally ill person therein named, personally at said hospital, on the .......... day of .......................... 19........

Sworn to and subscribed before me this
.......... day of .................... 19........

..........................................
Notary Public of New Jersey

My Commission Expires ......................

DR. FELDMAN:
Give this to pt. to keep.

1.

o o o

According to my memory, which could be a little off here, these are what I loved about Carrier:

The cigarette machines in the corridors.

Playing pool for hours at a full-size table in one of the day rooms. (The hospital also has an indoor basketball court; and a big, empty outdoor pool.)

Hanging out in the cute, cozy snack bar (a standalone structure in the middle of the hospital grounds serving sandwiches, malted milks, coffee and ice cream).

Having my bed made, laundry done and room cleaned by very nice hospital folks who don't seem to mind long-term exposure to crazy people.

My closest patient-buddy, a rich kid with a heroin history who has a great stereo system, shares his joints with me and licks his fingers after making it with a certain nurse in her car.

Recreational Therapy. I attend this often and with other patients learn to stain and decoupage blank wood boxes. I also learn how to make belts by carving designs into strips of leather and attaching fancy buckles (I gleefully and proudly make boxes and belts for most of my relatives, who don't seem to know what to do with them).

My daily doses of lithium carbonate. I am proudly part of some kind of big clinical trial of lithium, an agent Carrier shrinks, among others, view as a wonder drug—as the first viable way to stabilize manic-depressives, meaning it takes them off their highs, prevents future ones, and, some argue, stops depression as well. For the field of psychiatry, lithium is like all 7s on a Vegas slot.

My daily visits with a foxy woman doing research on lithium. She questions me at length regarding my mental and physical reactions to the drug. She makes me feel so cared about. I look at her and get aroused.

Three fine meals a day in a hotel-style dining room, where we sit in fancy Colonial chairs at big round tables and give our orders to patient, smiling, uniformed waitresses.

When my favorite Livingston professors and fellow students visit me. I love giving them a tour of the place, and chatting with them in one of our large, handsome lounges with expensive matching furniture and paintings of wild fowl.

Having groups of medical students interview me about manic-depression and lithium: I float in their attention, feel so smart, so articulate, so important.

Visits from Mercedes, a student at Douglass College (Rutgers). How the hell we met I don't remember, but she is a natural beauty with a keen intellect; she visits me one day wearing a leather miniskirt and black boots, we make-out in my room.

My sympathetic professors who give me extensions so that once I'm out I can make up missed coursework. That I complete a term paper on the Algerian revolution near the end of my Carrier stay shows I am beginning to care about reality again.

These are what I don't love about Carrier:

Seeing my staff psychiatrist almost daily in Doctor's House (a Colonial mansion converted into posh offices for the staff shrinks). I want to talk with him about my feelings, about sex, about human existence. All he cares about is how I'm doing on lithium. He is your basic pill-pusher, unwilling or unable to do cognitive ("talk") therapy.

Coming down. By my second month at Carrier, the lithium is working. I am stabilizing. Unfortunately, I'm now level enough to fully realize I am not at a country club and certainly not at Disneyland. I am a patient in a mental hospital and this is no joke. For the first time since my admission to Carrier, I am ashamed to be here. I want out.

# *"I LOST IT AT THE MOVIES"*

Pauline Kael, film critic, 1955.

I got out of Carrier around Christmas, 1970. I was on a ton of lithium and going back weekly to see my shrink on an outpatient basis. Among my lithium side-effects were diarrhea, a constant highly visible hand tremor and dry mouth. But my mania was gone—so gone that until spring I suffered from mild depression, chronic anxiety and the acute discomfort I felt when relatives, classmates and professors treated me gently or awkwardly, as if I were still a mental patient.

Even worse was the silent hurt and anger I felt when ostensibly close friends like Joel and Russell cracked jokes about my lithium. If I spoke or behaved in a way they deemed a little crazy, one of them would emphatically ask, "Uh, Eric, did you take your lithium today?" Then they'd chuckle.

At any rate, Mercedes and I had become a couple but she was gone for a semester abroad at Oxford (she'd arranged this long before we hooked up). I luckily had a few good friends on campus who knew about Carrier and didn't care, good people who treated me like a person, one of them.

Anyway, remember Marshall, the Livingston shrink who several months earlier had suggested I take a film-studies course during my junior year? Well, I did, and the truly brilliant professor who taught it and the movies he screened—by superb directors like Welles,

Hitchcock, Antonioni, Lubitsch, Bunuel—dazzled me with a form of art I'd never before considered a form of art.

I fell in love with film (manics are quick to fall in love, or what they think is love, with all sorts of phenomena). The low-level depression I'd been feeling steadily vanished and I happily discovered I had some talent for analyzing movies and writing about them. Funny, Mercedes and I not long after Carrier had seen the hit movie *Five Easy Pieces*, and afterward I told her at length what I thought about it. She told me I should be a film critic.

My passion for film now makes sense since movies are always moving. When I watched them I was moving with them in a fun, focused, dreamy, emotional and intellectual way—and to a large degree in a healthy way.

Nevertheless, my film thing wasn't unique back in 1971: College film-study courses were popping up all over the country and countless students were taking this new subject quite seriously. The only difference between me and most of them is that I rapidly went to the extreme by deciding, after less than a semester, that film criticism would be my career.

Also extreme was my often identifying with various screen characters. Consider: My first term paper for my Livingston film course was about "alienation" in three movies about troubled men.

And, needless to say, unlike most of my fellow film students, I was doing my usual transference, unconsciously viewing my terrific film professor and my favorite directors as good fathers, fathers I could praise, learn from and love.

o o o

That spring of 1971, Carrier monitored the amount of lithium in my body to keep it optimal. For the talk therapy I so wanted, the hospital referred me to Darrel, a psychiatrist whose office was near Livingston.

Darrel, unfortunately, seemed to know zero about talk therapy. Worse still, the moment I sat down in his office, he pressed the timer button on his desk clock. Hyperconscious of the clock's audible ticking and afraid my 50-minute session was running out, I paid more attention to the clock than to what I was trying to say about my thoughts and feelings; I stumbled over or mixed up lines and words, I felt hopelessly inarticulate and left each session sad and frustrated (I'd obviously suppressed my anger toward this father-authority figure; I should have smashed his fucking clock).

Worse still about Darrel, (this idiot, if you can believe it, was a Yale graduate, of course so was George W. Bush—says something about Yale back then)—worse still was his frequently telling me my father's check for his services hadn't arrived and insisting I make sure my father mail it on time. This dude, so obviously in medicine not to heal but rather to get rich, was too cheap to have a secretary or billing service, so he used me, and probably other patients, to ensure his revenue stream.

On the other hand, Darrel once caught my positive attention when he disagreed with Carrier's diagnosing me as manic-depressive; he said I was too young to be labeled with that disorder. (He was egregiously wrong; much recent psychiatric-pediatric research has discovered manic-depression all too often popping up in early childhood.) And I vaguely recall him saying I shouldn't be on lithium, which I liked hearing; I don't know why, save that I've heard manic-depressives on medication miss their highs. When I told him about my periods of post-Carrier depression, he urged me to go on antidepressants. I refused. I actually, stupidly thought I'd be "cheating" if I took them. This baffles me today: What insane mysticism was this? Whom, how or why the fuck did I think I'd be cheating?

Could manic-depressives like me secretly love their depressions?

At any rate, I did listen to Darrel about lithium—at the time I didn't want to be labeled as mentally ill, I wanted to see myself as "normal," I wanted everyone else to see me that way. And, I deduced, if I didn't take lithium, well, then, I wouldn't have manic-depression. Writer Joan Didion might call this "magical thinking."

As a result of such nonsense logic I subsequently told a shrink at Carrier, the guy running the lithium research, that I was going off lithium. He got angry, slapped his desk and growled, "You have had major manic episodes. If you go off lithium you will have more."

I went off it anyway. And he was right.

o o o

That same spring, thanks to a financial assist from my father, I was looking forward to a summer of traveling through Europe with Mercedes.

But as my departure neared, my anxiety about the trip and about my relationship with Mercedes shot way up and in time I had itchy ugly red rashes on my face and scalp. A dermatologist concluded I had seborrhea dermatitis—in my case, he said, it was a "neurodermatitis," that is, a stress-induced condition.

# GAINING ALTITUDE, LEVELING OFF

We're in June 1971. A prescription cream is suppressing my neurodermatitis, and I'm with Mercedes hitchhiking or taking trains across England and through a good part of Europe, including a romantic stay on an island in the Adriatic Sea off the coast of what was then Yugoslavia.

I felt a little happier each day. Mercedes and I were a good travel team, were enjoying each other more than ever, growing closer. Toward the end I thought I loved her, which was impossible because at the time I was incapable of loving anyone.

But I was quite capable of getting a bit too happy, too high. I should have realized this but did not realize this while we were in Venice, where I legally bought a big switchblade (and for the first five months of my senior year carried it concealed wherever I went on and off campus. I was paranoid about attackers. They never showed).

Mercedes and I said goodbye in Switzerland; she was returning to the States before summer's end to earn money for her senior year at Douglass. I then decided to hitch out of Switzerland and then across France and West Germany and part of East Germany to West Berlin.

I did. College kids were hitching all over Europe that summer, and I got rides with ease. Among my best road-trip memories: Spending a night alone in my sleeping bag deep inside Germany's mystical Black

Forest; sharing beer and Beatles music (from a portable record player) around a campfire next to the Rhine with German guys my age who kept talking in admiring tones about John F. Kennedy; really getting off on West Berlin and the Wall, Checkpoint Charlie, East Berlin; and finally hitching back across both Germanys to Amsterdam and a plane home.

o o o

I was pretty high when I returned to Livingston for my senior year. But I was lucky: I stayed on a hypomanic plateau all year, never soaring into mania or sliding into depression.

And despite all my other psycho-trash, I managed to vector into film study all the energy and intellectual acuity that come with hypomania. I took every film course each division of Rutgers offered that year; wrote numerous film reviews for Livingston's newspaper; had my first scholarly film article accepted for publication; got accepted for graduate film study at UCLA, my first choice because of its reputation as the best film school in the country; won a coveted Danforth Fellowship to pay for graduate school; and spent most of my nights with Mercedes in her apartment. This was a heady time.

o o o

I didn't attend my Livingston graduation. I was angry at the school for a variety of reasons. This was so stupid and ungrateful since no other college I can think of would have put up with me. I mean, if you're going to go crazy in college, Livingston was the place to do it.

But I needed many years to see that. And in lieu of wearing a cap and gown, I spent my 1972 graduation day and most of May and June with a new girlfriend at her parents' summer home in rural-rich Connecticut. (I adored her and admired her and loved our sex; still, I was set on eventually leaving her for California. I told her so before we got involved, and for her own reasons she accepted this short-term liaison.)

o o o

For the record: Despite what I viewed as Livingston's flaws, my superlative professors there—combined with the high-yield courses I'd had at NYU—gave me an all-around undergraduate education superior to that of any student I'd soon meet in grad school.

# FLUFF

I next spent six happy weeks at the Santa Cruz, California home of a close friend from Livingston. I only mention this because he more than once complimented me, saying that of the many house guests he'd had that summer, I was the only one he didn't have to keep entertained around the clock. He liked my leaving the house every day and going off on my own for hours to bookstores, coffee shops, the beach.

I didn't tell him I spent so many hours alone because I was essentially a loner: I could not be with other people no matter who they were, no matter how kind and smart (like him) for more than a few waking hours. My social-anxiety level always shot up five or more points when I was with other people (except certain lovers)—I always, finally, had to get away, be alone. I was happiest alone.

So much so that I left Santa Cruz a month early, drove my Plymouth Fury down the Pacific Coast Highway, got my first L.A. apartment and then worked as a messenger, a job that crash-coursed me in the city's spectacular and thrilling, for me at least, grid of freeways and surface streets. I was getting high, but I stayed in control, looking forward to UCLA.

Mercedes arrived in L.A., got her own apartment, enrolled in grad school at USC. We started up again. And with much energy and optimism I that September started my graduate film studies.

o o o

Put simply, UCLA turned out to be one of my best colossal mistakes.

First off, my bitter recall tells me that UCLA at the time did not have what far too many people erroneously called a "film school." Fact is UCLA did not even have a "film department." What it had back then in the fall of 1972 was a Department of Theater Arts (with a program for aspiring actors); plus a dismal, skeletal Motion Picture/Television Division (production only) with a faculty mostly made up of washouts from the "industry"—the industry being the visible and invisible people who actually finance, create, manage and otherwise have a hand in commercial film and TV; and, finally, tucked into a few offices and some squalid seminar rooms you find the never-never land of the "Critical Studies [film-criticism] Program," which has access to an adjacent, first-rate movie theater more than not showing second-rate films.

This was my Master of Arts program (what became a fraudulent Ph.D. curriculum wasn't even in place when I arrived). And the M.A. thing, supposedly devoted to film criticism, history and theory, was in reality dedicated only to perpetuating its own incredible mediocrity. Its Olympian reputation had no basis in fact.

Indeed, the Critical Studies faculty was quite small and only one of its professors had a feel for—or, arguably, any interest in—teaching. The lower-level instructors were at best woefully incompetent; one was brain-dead.

Livingston professors I'd liked and respected had unknowingly advised me to attend UCLA on the basis of fluff: Seems they'd all heard about UCLA's film school and heard about its great facilities and heard about its ties to the industry. But none of them had ever verified any of this.

No one knew that the chairman of the film-studies program and my initial M.A. advisor, Woodrow, was a manipulative, sadistic nut-case whose ignorance about film was exponentially greater than his knowledge of it. I mean, this guy was film-challenged.

No one knew that Rutgers University, in New Brunswick, N.J. of all places, was offering film courses light years ahead of the crap I ran into at UCLA.

In a matter of weeks, I was disillusioned, frustrated, angry, despondent. I swirled down from hypomania into a mixed state and then into what I knew was depression. I knew because I was crying every night alone in my apartment. I knew because I could feel the mounting moments of sadness, terror and paralysis.

Mercedes, meantime, like my father and other people, wasn't terribly tolerant of my depression. "That's because," a shrink later told me, "they fear their own capacity for depression; what we hate in others is what we hate in ourselves."

During this and earlier depressions, people often told me—no, ordered me—to "snap out of it." They did not and still don't understand this fact: No one simply "snaps out"of clinical depression.

Oh well, Mercedes that autumn did her best to help me. She took me, for instance, to a big museum in downtown L.A. I'd never been there, and I followed her, zombie-like, through the exhibit halls. She tried so hard to be my cheerleader. Didn't work. Never does.

But when we got to a room filled with all kinds of guns in big cases, I broke through my zero-emotion trance (shrinks call it "flat affect") and I pressed my face against case after case of muskets, rifles, revolvers, pistols, derringers and hundreds of other firearms from all over history. While studying all the fine craftsmanship of these weapons, I kept happily blurting, "Mercedes, Wow! Jesus! Look at these!" Mercedes was not interested in guns, but she seemed relieved and happy to see me so excited.

Didn't last. Back at her apartment, the gun room faded and so did I.

o o o

Severely depressed by Christmas, I flew home, where my alarmed father had me see the shrink who'd treated me at Carrier. I told him what was happening, and he said he wanted to put me on imipramine (generic Tofranil), an antidepressant medication, which, he said, would only need from one to three weeks to kick in.

After the guy gave me a sample bottle of imipramine, he told me to start seeing a shrink in L.A. on a regular basis because the drug could cause mania. I was so down I didn't hear him. And if he mentioned my going back on lithium I didn't hear that either. Maybe I was secretly waiting to get high again.

Nine months later, I asked a psychiatrist I'd been seeing at UCLA's student health center to put me back on lithium because I'd gotten a speeding ticket and was worried about getting high again; she obliged, but we soon stopped it because the absurd, painful demands of my M.A. program, especially researching and writing a required Master's thesis that at any other school would have qualified as a Ph.D. dissertation, made an anti-mania drug unnecessary. Around this time I began taking Valium for insomnia, and continued to do so for the next decade or so (after which a shrink switched me to anti-anxiety Xanax, and a subsequent shrink replaced that with Klonopin).

You see, despite imipramine, I was stuck in a mixed state of fear, bitterness, anger and hate—all involving Woodrow and his fucking program. And yet I somewhat miraculously streamed all this emotion into compulsive-obsessive work on my thesis, a 267-page document

I'm still proud of. Its title: "Wars of Perception: Selected Studies in American World War II Documentary Film."

My fairly extensive research for the thing included six weeks in Washington, D.C. I virtually camped out at the National Archives, which had many of the documentaries I wanted to study (on the institution's viewing machines) and write about. Thus, in the name of film scholarship, I was happily reliving my childhood fascination with war.

And war was still tugging at me because, as I've noted, it almost perfectly mimicked my lifetime conflict with my father and people like him—and, most important, its hatred, violence, fury, terror, sadness, triumphant elation and across-the-board-loss almost perfectly mimic manic-depression.

That I would want to revisit manic-depression in any way on one hand astounds me and on the other in no way surprises me. I suspect I secretly love the illness. In a skewed way, it gives me an identity. Makes me feel special.

o o o

The fine psychiatrist who treated me at UCLA in 1973 and 1974, after hearing me talk about my pleasing-rebellious-child behavior, suggested I try what was for me a new form of group therapy called "assertion training" (or "behavior modification"). I did, participating weekly in one group, and the next year in another.

I enjoyed "behavior mod." We told our upbeat, bright therapists about disturbing personal behaviors we wanted to change—and in the course of helping us, they'd have us repeatedly role-play (realistically act out, as if on stage) various social or interpersonal situations that sent our stress levels into the stratosphere. In my case, for example, I was upset about, among other things, my timidity in restaurants. Mercedes and I were eating out a lot; I'd be in the middle of trying to make a selection from the menu when a waiter or waitress would appear and ask if we were ready to order. I most often wasn't ready to order, but was always afraid to say so and ask for more time; instead I'd panic and order a dish I wasn't sure I really wanted. (You see, transference again, I viewed all service people, among so many others, from waiters to auto mechanics to physicians, as father-or mother-figures; I wanted them to love me, and I was afraid they'd punish me if I didn't please them.)

In response to my restaurant problem, the therapists taught me to hold up my hand, spread my fingers and politely but assertively say, "I'd like five more minutes, please." We acted this out over and over, with one of the therapists role-playing a restaurant waiter, and I sitting at an imaginary table reading a menu. I think we also switched roles; I played the waiter, and the therapist used the "five-minutes" line, which reinforced my learning it.

I subsequently used this new behavior every time I was at a restaurant and wasn't ready to order when asked. It always worked. The waiter or waitress would invariably respond with something like "Okay, sure, let me know when you're ready."

This and other self-assertion techniques I learned in both groups were a tremendous help to me and boosted my self-esteem. But only in the specific situations where I used them. You see, the therapists thought that the positive techniques we patients learned in terms of social interaction would generalize to all of our behaviors, and in turn change for the better how we felt about ourselves.

This never happened in my case. I became a pro at stuff like restaurant-ordering, but overall, I remained a psychosocial mess soon to be more manic-depressive than ever.

# "PLEASE KNOCK LOUDLY"

I have by June 1974 spent six very rough years in college, coping with my madness while trying to earn my degrees. After getting my Master's I meet with a UCLA career counselor who tells me the only chance I have of getting a job in my field is to "leave town."

I still loved L.A. and wanted to stay and stupidly believed that given my strong academic record, book-quality M.A. thesis and three articles published in scholarly film journals—well, Christ, certainly some film-related company would hire me for research or writing or whatever. Besides, I wasn't asking for much, just my foot in the proverbial door.

Problem was: so were countless thousands of other people in L.A. and all over the country. Moreover, I had no "contacts," no industry people who could give me a vital assist. And so I collided with the steel-reinforced-concrete truth that all my achievements in college had nothing to do with making it in the industry.

After two months of trying and failing to get at this point any kind of media-related position, I finally, after passing a fucking typing test and doing my best during three interviews, landed a job at CBS Television City in Los Angeles, a huge production facility where hit shows like "All in the Family" were taped before live audiences—where for eight hours a day, as a "senior clerk" in the audience-relations department, I typed onto envelopes the addresses of people who'd called or written us for tickets to shows, and then I stuffed the requested tickets into the envelopes.

At first I was euphoric over getting this mindless job: I thought I could quickly move up at CBS into something I'd like and do well at, like script-evaluation or program analysis.

Never happened. I applied for all kinds of promising jobs inside the company, and got none. When I interviewed with one executive and offered to show him my Master's thesis—he laughed. End of interview.

While failing to transcend my clerical job, I grew to hate it, the boredom, the idiot work. "I didn't spend six years in college to stuff tickets into envelopes," I bitterly told myself and others. And in time I hated CBS and by extension all corporate media for ignoring me. (Manic-depressives often fail to see how insignificant they are. How can you when you're the center of your own universe?)

So I quit cold, leaving me unemployed and again looking for work. Fuck the media, I'll take any employer who wants me.

I was in a mixed-state of frenzy and lethargy, but I thought I was normal. And I applied for a job at the Central Intelligence Agency.

o o o

Since my James-Bond-fixated early teens, some of my favorite reading had been about espionage. John Le Carre's elegant spy novels seduced me, as did various histories of the CIA.

In fact, I was reading a Le Carre book near the end of my CBS debacle and falling a little too much in love with the subsurface world of "spookdom"—secret government intelligence agencies.

Conveniently forgetting all my anti-capitalist and Vietnam-protest days, I thought, quite delusionally, that the CIA (aka the"Company") would value me as an analyst of Soviet news and entertainment media, or something like that.

Maybe the agency thought so too; I don't know. But after calling their number (they actually had one listed in the L.A. phone book) for information and then sending them a resume, I got myself invited to a CIA office near the main L.A. airport.

I remember showing up at a numbered door inside an anonymous office building. The door had no agency logo; it was blank, save for a tiny strip of print beneath a peephole that said, "Please knock loudly."

I am thrilled. I am about to enter spookdom. After I knock loudly, an elderly lady without a word lets me in and motions to another office door; I gently knock and a voice tells me to enter.

And for the next hour or more, an older man, who never gives me his name, who's smoking a pipe behind a big bare desk, a nice almost jocular guy, talks with me about politics, foreign policy and certain U.S. defense contractors, which he dismissively notes are "sucking" the government dry of money—and what do I think about that? Of course I agree with him and recite my own analysis of government-corporate relations and how some companies are "traitorous." He seems to like my answer. Which strikes me as odd: I have always viewed the CIA's primary mission as the furtherance of U.S. corporate (neocapitalist) expansionism worldwide.

Whatever the case, he ends our talk by giving me a long application to fill out at home, and he pushes a large, laminated sheet of paper in front of me, silently indicating I should read it. The laminated document tells me, in essence, that I agree under penalty of federal law never to disclose a single detail of my current and future contact with the CIA—to say nothing about it to no one, not even my spouse if I have one. I think I then signed something.

At home, I spent hours on the application, trying to give the Company what I thought it wanted to hear about me. I knew I wasn't qualified to be what I'd heard was called a "case officer," someone who hires, trains, manages and pays the folks who actually do the Company's dirty work. No, what I did was to showcase myself as a highly educated media analyst. I highlighted all of my academic achievements and inflated my CBS job into what sounded like a junior-executive position in public relations. And, needless to say, I had absolutely no psychiatric record, no arrest record. I knew from reading that the CIA was always paranoid about the "opposition" successfully blackmailing one of its members into revealing U.S. secrets. Meaning people with nasty personal histories to hide (sexual, financial, legal, psychiatric) need not apply.

I also knew from somewhere that if they really wanted me, they'd do a full background check and easily uncover my entire crazy past. This worried me until my friend Trevor, who'd been an Army intelligence officer under deep cover in Thailand, told me to lie about my past until I got to the "wire"—until they hooked me up to a lie detector.

Trevor said some people could "beat the wire," but warned I shouldn't try. He advised me to admit Rochester and Carrier but to explain those episodes away as the typical behavior of a confused college kid who, misdiagnosed as manic-depressive, needed to find his identity. Given my all-star academic performance, he noted, and given my applying to be an office-bound intelligence analyst, not a covert-operations "cowboy" mounting right-wing coups in Central America, I had a good chance of making it. Besides, he said, the Company was filled with crazy people.

By now I really wanted in.

Shortly after returning my completed application I received a spooky letter (no return address, no letterhead, no signature, no mention of the CIA) telling me to report in two weeks to a local college campus.

I did, and spent a morning taking math-and verbal-aptitude tests. About 30 other candidates were there too. No one talked to anyone else during the coffee break, ditto after we finished. We all acted like spooks. I'm not even sure the people handing out and collecting the tests ever spoke to us. Weird.

Unfortunately, I had the flu and could barely concentrate and thus probably blew the tests, which I guess is why the CIA never again contacted me. I blamed myself for this, and yet I was secretly relieved, as if I'd "dodged a bullet," as if some remnant of sanity in me knew full well that the Company was bad news.

o o o

I survived the next few months by registering with one of L.A.'s several "office temp" (employment) agencies and then doing part-time clerical work for various companies around town. I had fun. The work helped me inch up from a mixed-state into borderline hypomania.

Most regrettably, I also during this period fell into a three-month heavy rescue game with Ami, a UCLA coed, friend and neighbor. I played the sensitive, supportive rescuer. She, to the hilt, played the victim. Like others who play this role, she embraced her victimhood, her tsuris: She talked, whined, agonized nonstop about her daily pain and suffering at the awful hands of the married professor she was sleeping with, or the bisexual actor she wanted to sleep with, or the songwriter who dumped her, or her control-freak tyrannical mother, or her mechanically challenged Jaguar, or the universe in general.

We played about five evenings a week. She would normally ask me over, turn on some music, serve me white wine and a few times make me supper. She often changed from her school outfit into a yellow negligee over her bra and panties. I don't quite know why she did this since any sex feelings between victim and rescuer are so suppressed they don't exist—if not the game explodes like a supernova.

I once tried to "reality-check" Ami by asking her if she felt any romantic attraction to me. She said no. I dropped it right there and asked her about her latest fight with her mother.

Anyway, in mid-May, I finally played what I called the "Ami Card." You see Ami's father was a TV producer reasonably well-known and influential in certain sectors of the industry. My savings were exhausted, I told Ami, I couldn't find work (both were true by then), could she ask her father if he could help me—only if she wanted to ask him, of course. (This brief role-reversal, me asking her help for once, actually keeps the game going; it slows down the unconscious but growing tensions and resentments endemic to the game.)

It worked. Thanks to Ami and her father, I found myself a week later interviewing with an industry insider, a successful TV producer of network documentaries. He gave me a tryout by assigning me the script research for one of his upcoming documentary series about African wildlife. He only gave me four days to do what would have normally taken me weeks, but I punched in my afterburners and with little sleep met his deadline.

He liked my writing and research, told me he was so impressed he was seriously thinking about hiring me as a full-time writer-researcher.

I blew it. The tremendous energy I'd plowed into his report had pushed me from hypomania up into mania. So when the guy mentions hiring me, I stupidly, arrogantly, maniacally tell him, "No, I don't want a staff job, but I'll take you on as my client."

Seems that somewhere during the Ami game—which by the way ended when I got intensely, romantically and sexually involved with another woman—somewhere during the game I'd decided I wanted to become a "media consultant," like some of the high-paid communications gurus I'd read about or had seen interviewed on TV. I thought I was perfect for the consulting business and could launch my own firm. Once more, I'd lost touch. I didn't see that the big shots I admired had worked long and hard for years to get where they were.

Back to the "client" stuff: The producer says okay, I can work for him on a freelance (independent contractor) basis. And so I began six months of heady work for him. I thought I was so cool, finally inside the industry. I was manic, but my tough assignments and stiff deadlines kept me anchored. But not completely: I imagined I was making a fortune when in fact I was only getting $125 per report.

Crazily thinking I was getting rich, I applied for, got and abused numerous credit and charge cards. When card applications asked about employment, I billed myself as the "President" of my own media-consulting firm. This was all delusional, crazy.

Like most manics I was unspeakably terrible with money. Plastic in hand, I did typical manic things like becoming a regular shopper at Beverly Hills high-status stores like Saks Fifth Avenue, charging up lots of expensive clothing and exotic men's cologne from Paris, that sort of nonsense. I also fulfilled a latent fantasy from childhood by opening a charge account at a Beverly Hills sporting-goods store and buying a Walther PPK semiautomatic pistol, the James Bond weapon, and, I was told, the standard-issue handgun at the CIA. (I think the California firearms-purchase application I had to fill out asked about psychiatric problems; I wrote that I had none).

My mania was full-blast. I took an armed-combat course with an ex-Marine ex-cop who owned his own shooting range. He taught me a lot about guns and how to use them; he was crazy, but so was I, and we got along quite well.

My libido, meanwhile, as with most manics, was voracious. Which is why I dove into a number of short, doomed love affairs.My libido, meanwhile, as with most manics, was voracious, which is why I dove into a number of short, doomed love affairs...

Along with lots of sex, I stepped-up my credit-card abuse with stuff like flying down to Mexico City on a bizarre trip to find "clients" and then from there flying up to D.C. and with the help of a good connection getting a $1,600 contract to write a bicycle safety booklet for a federal agency. I wrote the piece, got paid, thought I was a millionaire, and rocketed higher to nowhere.

o o o

Lost in my own manic solar system, I insanely felt I finally had a real identity; I felt strong, manly and cool, and saw myself physically attractive to women (extremely rare for me)—especially because after the Walther PPK, I bought a muscle car, a 1970 Dodge Challenger 383 Magnum RT/SE.

I named my car "Maria," after the heroine-antiheroine of Joan Didion's novel, *Play It As It Lays*, whose problems and perceptions I identified with.

Manics drive maniacally, and in 1975 I racked up lots of tickets. So many that the state Department of Motor Vehicles put me on three year's probation, saying one more ticket and they'd revoke my license. I became the most timid, law-abiding driver in L.A.

Nearly 20 years later, I was so broke I sold my Challenger to a collector. I've been a fulltime pedestrian and bus rider ever since; I've come to enjoy not owning a car, not having to worry about and pay for things like fuel, insurance, parts and repairs. Perhaps my car-less life, in today's age of human-induced, planet-threatening climate change, is a mark of sanity.

o o o

A mixed-state and then major depression caught up with me by January 1976. I gave up on my own "company" and worked for a film festival and then an independent film producer. Both jobs I hated and quit after a few months.

Then I stopped trying to find a decent job. To survive, I sold or pawned most of my possessions; and I once again got a temporary office job, this time at a huge magazine corporation. It was pure idiot work—typing form letters and updating mailing lists—and even this I found almost impossible, thanks to my having shot down into depression's silent hysteria and crippling anxiety, self-hate and despair.

So there I was, for the next six months trying to function in a big bleak room above a shoddy stretch of Sunset Boulevard, sitting there with some 35 other clerks, all teenaged girls. I never spoke to them, nor they to me, not even a "Good morning." I think the supervisor kept me on because she knew I was mentally ill and felt sorry for me. I'll never know.

What I do know is that I sat there every day waiting to see Angie that night.

## *"Good morning heartache. Here we go again..."*

Irene Higgenbothom, Ervin Drake and Dan Fisher
(Decca Records), 1946.

Angie. Let me backtrack for a second.

On finishing my Master's and leaving UCLA in the summer of 1974, and thus no longer qualifying for free meds and psychotherapy from the school's student health service, I went to the Los Angeles Free Clinic for help. The clinic's psychiatrist supplied me with imipramine and I joined a therapy group that met weekly. Our group leader, Angie, was a bright, articulate, attractive woman perhaps in her early 50s; alternately firm, funny, lucid, pissed-off, piercing, tender, vulgar, Angie had a good feel for the what, how and why of human emotion and behavior. I most always listened very closely to what she said, tried to memorize it. And yet my manic-depression and attendant personality problems remained in place. Immune to her first-rate therapy, I stayed stuck in my mad thinking and behavior, whether I was high, low or drifting between the two. This held true no matter what Angie tried with me.

I don't remember exactly how this got started, but for five months beginning in early 1976, I went to Angie's home every night. We were alone together (she and her husband were separated). She sometimes made me dinner, and she always served me wine; a few glasses of it, coupled with her attentive words, would calm me. Before I left, we always hugged, no, embraced. My demons wouldn't return until the next morning.

Before the wine and background music like Billie Holiday, we would "work." This meant she would be the therapist and I the patient. I generally said the same thing every night, simply rearranging words and topics, crying whenever I mentioned a former girlfriend or how much I missed all the possessions I'd desperately sold or, worse still, had for no logical reason thrown out a few months earlier.

After this therapy session, we'd converse like normal people; the only problem was that our talk always seemed to tilt back toward me. When she shared one of her problems with me, I didn't want to hear it. I didn't have room for her pain. When I'm that depressed (or manic) I only have acreage for me. I want your full attention all the time.

Once I get all your attention, I will twist it and spin it—I will take it to mean you love me. Or hate me. How I take you in has nothing to do with you but stems purely from my own sickness.

Angie gave me all of her attention. And I sucked it down as if I were a black hole in her living room. And, get this, despite her being the therapist who taught me all about the rescue game and its horrific dangers, she and I fell into that damn game ourselves, with she the savior, me the victim.

My persecutors?

I had a universe of them, but I myself was the meanest, ugliest of them all (I think this is common among heavy depressives). I constantly told her how much I hated myself—and then told her how much I hated myself for hating myself. I sometimes brought up suicide.

Immersed in victimhood, I didn't realize we were playing neurotic roles. But looking back, I think Angie knew what we were doing. I think she used every tool she had to end it, but failed.

o o o

I was once telling her how much time I spent thinking about her while I was at work during the day. She stopped me, saying, "You sound obsessed with me, as if you're in love with me. Are you?"

"Jesus,"I thought. I saw Angie as the mother I wanted, needed, never had. And at the time, March 1976, she was the only person in my otherwise empty, dead life.

I tried to tell her love had never entered my frame of reference toward her, or anyone else. She nodded. Then she said, "You know, I thought about making love with you—but I didn't think you could handle it."

I agreed. I don't want your body, I thought, I want your love. And I won't give you a thing in return.

o o o

During this depression, as in earlier ones, I often panicked about all kinds of nonsense. But my panic over the bills I couldn't pay was well-grounded. I was looking at several thousand bucks of debt courtesy of my manic, 1975 plastic-abuse.

And thus, with help from my attorney-cousin Elliot, who lived in the L.A. high-income district of Encino, I filed for and was granted full protection from my creditors under Chapter 7 of the U.S. Bankruptcy Code. This entailed my completing a heap of legal and financial forms and, despite my absolute terror of doing so, my appearing in federal court.

The courtroom, as Elliot had predicted, was jammed with depressed and depressing bankruptcy applicants like me. When I was finally called to take the witness stand, a federal official quickly leafed through my application, and then asked if I had any remaining property of value. I told him I had a small AM/FM radio, he smiled a little—and that was it: I was on and off the stand in what felt like 60 seconds, which is what Elliot had also predicted.

To be sure, the entire bankruptcy process was a bit more involved, but what matters here is that I left the courtroom debt-free. What happened is that the federal court, in essence, tells all the folks to whom you owe money to go fuck themselves. The only problem was that my credit-rating was now zilch, forcing me over the next eight years to live mobster-style: cash only, of if someone trusted me, a personal check. (Oh, by the way, personal bankruptcy these days is reportedly much harder due to changes in the law.)

o o o

A month or so after the bankruptcy, I applied to UCLA for readmission to get a Ph.D. in film studies (the doctoral film program was now finally in place). When I told Angie, she was startled, "I thought you were miserable there," she said. "You told me you hated it."

I responded with some garbage about how I'd finally realized I was an academic at heart and belonged on a college campus. The truth I didn't tell her was that I feared I had nowhere else on Earth to go.

In the meantime, Andrew, the only UCLA film professor I'd ever both liked and learned from, got me back into my old program and also arranged for me to be a paid teaching assistant (a doctoral student who works for a professor by leading student discussion groups and grading papers). What's more, the Danforth Foundation reinstated my fellowship. This generous award, as with my Master's, would pay my tuition and part of my living expenses.

I clearly remember, after these good things happened, looking up at the Hollywood Hills from my living room and thinking: "I'm saved."

o o o

I was still seeing Angie while Andrew was paving my way back to grad school, we're in the spring of 1976. Now Angie was one of those therapists who opposed the use of medication to treat disordered personalities like mine. She knew my mental history, but she rejected Carrier's label of manic-depression. She argued that people like me could change their feelings, thinking and behavior and in time, if they worked at it, feel better, even happy, about themselves and their lives—assuming they truly wanted to let go of their pain. Meds, she said, only suppress feelings, get in the way of treatment and recovery, do nothing to solve the structural problems.

I believed her, and, as I'd done five years earlier, rejected Carrier's diagnosis. However I stayed stuck in my depression; instead of recovering I got worse, suicidal. And by late May, Angie gave up on me. She never said that. But she finally suggested I go back on my former antidepressant, imipramine.

I did. Unfortunately, I didn't go back on anti-mania lithium. And, you guessed it, in less than a month I went from clinical depression into a mixed-state and by July, for the first time in seven months, I felt happy.

And by July, too, I'd stopped seeing Angie, instead doing stuff—bars, movies, restaurants, night clubs and the like—with friends I'd earlier abandoned. Angie had predicted this after I went back on imipramine: "Once you feel better again," she said, "the iron wall will come down between us." Not long after saying this, she moved back in with her husband in Orange County and got me out of her life.

When she left, I felt relieved. The game was over.

About this time, my neighbor-friend Samantha and I regularly sunned ourselves on a beach near Malibu and at night went to Studio One, a huge, glitzy gay disco in West Hollywood where we danced for hours. I had no romantic interest in Samantha nor she with me; no, we spent most of our conversation time playing a low-key rescue game with me the rescuer. What else is new?

More trips to the beach, more disco, stir in my fucked-up DNA, and by August I was so happy I swirled up into hypomania. By September I was once again manic, only more so than ever before.

# CRASH LANDING

I cannot believe—no, I can believe—how easily I conned myself and others into thinking I was eager to resume UCLA after my first sickening time there.

Sure enough, I only needed a few weeks to get angry at the film-studies program, which was, unbelievably, worse than two years earlier. I hated the moron professor I worked for, and I was beyond hatred, if that's possible, when it came to Woodrow, who was still the same smug, Nazi asshole.

This fall of 1976 was also when I purchased my first Colt .45 semiautomatic pistol, along with a holster, spare clip and other accessories, plus a Gerber Mark II killing knife. This was when I started going to that big outdoor firing range in the San Fernando Valley.

Beware: Guns and my kind of mania go together. From boyhood to my mid-20s, I loved guns. They were a perfect way to compensate for my profound feelings of across-the-board weakness—they were also a profound way to express my conscious and unconscious rage at enemies real and imaged.

People like me should not be allowed to have guns.

# FOR THE BIRDS

For Thanksgiving 1976, I drove 600 miles north of L.A. to Bodega Bay, about 65 miles up the coast from San Francisco. I chose this scenic, almost mystical fishing hamlet in Sonoma County because Alfred Hitchcock used it in one of my favorite movies of his, *The Birds.*

Once there, I reveled in seeing the buildings and streets I'd seen in the movie, and I eagerly questioned local people who'd watched the filming. Outside of town, I drove around aimlessly, my loaded Colt .45 on the front passenger seat.

The weekend spurred my manic elation. Why not? I was on imipramine without lithium, a serious mistake, like driving without a steering wheel.

When Sunday evening came, I raced back to L.A. I kept my loaded Colt and my Gerber knife next to me on the passenger seat. In my trunk I had 300 rounds of ammunition and two books: a one-volume encyclopedia called *Small Arms of the World*; and a book titled *Secrets of Modern Knife Fighting*, its text and photos teaching readers various ways to kill people with a combat knife.

Anyway, I hit L.A. and got off the freeway around 1 a.m. and headed for home through the upscale Westwood district of the city, normally a safe neighborhood, but at the time, I later learned, the scene of some armed robberies that had left its residents terrified. Moreover, I think someone later told me my car matched the one the bad guy was supposedly using.

COPY

IN THE MUNICIPAL COURT OF LOS ANGELES JUDICIAL DISTRICT

COUNTY OF LOS ANGELES, STATE OF CALIFORNIA

---o---

HON. DAVID PEREZ, JUDGE DIVISION NO. 90

| | |
|---|---|
| THE PEOPLE OF THE STATE OF CALIFORNIA, Plaintiff, | No. 753,374 |
| -vs- | VIOLATION OF: |
| | SECTION 12031(a) PC COUNT I |
| | SECTION 12020 PC COUNT II |
| ERIC MICHAEL KRUEGER, | SECTION 22350 VC COUNT III |
| Defendant. | MISDEMEANORS |

---o---

REPORTER'S TRANSCRIPT OF PROCEEDINGS

Thursday, February 10, 1977

---o---

APPEARANCES:

For the Plaintiff: BURT PINES
City Attorney
BY: SAMUEL EATON
Deputy City Attorney

For the Defendant: STANLEY W. W. KESSELMAN
Attorney at Law
8530 Wilshire Boulevard
4th Floor
Beverly Hills, California 90211
(213) 659-2611

LOUISE A. EAHEART, CSR
Official Reporter
Certificate No. 1277

Okay, so I've driven barely a mile when an LAPD (Los Angeles Police Department) patrol car stops me. Given my previous traffic stops when manic, I know the drill. Two cops walk up, one on each side of my car, and the cop on my side asks for my license and registration and says I was speeding. I say, "I'm sorry, officer. I didn't realize it." Then I feel compelled to add, in the most polite tone I can use, "Officer, by the way, I have an unconcealed, loaded Colt .45 automatic on the seat next to me."

I insanely think he'll say, "Gee, thanks for telling me son, may I see the papers for it?"

Wrong.

The cop freaks out, draws his revolver and aims at my head, screaming over and over "Freeze! Hands out of the car! Get out!"

Meantime, his partner on the other side of my car is also freaking out and pointing his gun at my head and screaming into a walkie-talkie; sure enough, as I very slowly exit my car and feel the hard steel handcuffs click around my wrists, I see a pack of black-and-whites, their sirens and lights hysterical, racing toward me.

These guys thought they had the armed robber Westwood's well-heeled residents wanted dead. However all they told me was that I was under arrest for having a loaded gun in my car; they didn't bother with Miranda; they impounded my car and shoved me into one of theirs.

Remember, I was totally manic, and thus for a few minutes, as during my Rochester arrest, I enjoyed the whole experience, I liked being the center of so much official attention. But by the time we got to LAPD's West Los Angeles lockup, I was pissed-off over having my trip interrupted—especially after I'd been so polite and disclosive about the Colt. I got angrier during booking and angrier still when they put me in a large cell with about 20 other guys. Worried about being hassled or attacked, I tried to act very tough, although I soon realized my cell-mates were harmless. One of them told me he'd been arrested for jaywalking.

Now I wanted out, pronto. I finally got my one allowed phone call and reached my Encino-attorney-cousin Elliot. I think he liked me either because of my illness or despite my illness or possibly because I wrote well and he secretly wanted to quit law and become some sort of "creative," an actor, a novelist, whatever, anything but corporate law.

At any rate, Elliot bailed me out and drove me home and told me about my upcoming arraignment and how he'd handle it. As I got out of his car and thanked him a few thousand times, he smiled and said, "You know, Eric, nice Jewish boys don't carry guns."

I was in court a few days later with Elliot beside me. First, he entered what I thought was a clever plea of "nolo contendere" (we accept the charge, will take the punishment, but won't admit guilt). Then, before sentencing, Elliot told the judge all about my stellar scholarship at Rutgers and UCLA and how he and I had grown up together in New Jersey (lie) and what a nice, harmless guy I was, and, get this, I only had a gun and 300 rounds of ammo in my car because I'd gone to Sonoma County to do a lot of target practice—and, also, my neighborhood has recently had several break-ins (lie). Elliot was at his cogent, mild-mannered courtroom best. The judge, who could have jailed me, let me off with a $95 fine and a year's probation. He allowed the police to confiscate my Colt and my Gerber.

Didn't matter. I soon used a chunk of my Danforth money to buy another Colt .45 semiautomatic, a Bianchi quick-draw shoulder-holster and a Gerber Mark I double-edged dagger with a sheath I could clip onto my belt or inside my cowboy boot. I wore cowboy boots back then, thought they made me cool, manly.

o o o

I shot up further after the Thanksgiving arrest into manic-psychosis. I was off the proverbial grid. Out of the envelope. An F-15 in a vertical climb. Superman! I miraculously dodged legal troubles until, two months after Thanksgiving, I went a little berserk. Still a UCLA doctoral student and a teaching assistant, I consistently disrupted my graduate seminars with diatribes about the universe. As with most manics, my speech was pressured and driven by a flight of ideas. When I wasn't making crazy speeches, I verbally attacked my fellow seminar students and disrupted whatever my professors were trying to do, and denounced the entire Ph.D. program.

As for my teaching job, I told the students in my discussion group I hated traditional grading systems and in protest would give everyone an A for the quarter. Grades and standardized-test scores, I heatedly told them, were merely ways to measure someone's ability to get high grades and high test scores and had nothing to do with learning, teaching, intelligence, creativity—and were major contributors to America's socioeconomic inequality, which our neocapitalist system demands. Frankly, I still believe this. But several higher-ups at UCLA did not, and I caught a lot of flack.

My mania at this point was in part a cyclonic paranoid rage at anything I deemed my enemy. Woodrow I deemed one of my worst enemies; I still hated him for the sadistic way he'd treated me during the two years of my Master's program. And now in 1977, I was increasingly and more openly at war with him.

My worst and funniest attack on the guy came early in 1977 when I had to take his seminar on "Surrealism and Film." That the arrogant prick didn't know anything about surrealism—and, as I noted, was film-challenged to begin with—only made me angrier, and crazier.

So when he ordered each of us to prepare a 90-minute lecture on a topic of our choice related to surrealism, I put together an insane slide show and analytic narrative of surrealist architecture. In the course of my research, I learned that some surrealists when performing in a theater fired real guns in the air. I decided to mimic them and to be as outrageous and infuriating as possible to fuck-up Woodrow's brain.

Okay, so now I'm sitting in a seminar room at a big table with my fellow doctoral students. Woodrow is also at the table, frowning. My turn to lecture comes. While showing my slides and talking, I start doing weird things with objects I take out of a big cardboard box I'd brought with me. I throw rubber rats and spiders all over the room and run a toy racing car across the seminar table. Then I brandish a display model (a perfect but nonoperational replica) of a German World War II Schmeisser MP40 submachine gun. I yank back the weapon's firing bolt, which makes a very ominous sound, and point the barrel at various kids in the room. They are visibly scared. Through all this and more zany stuff, I keep talking about surrealist architecture and show more slides.

I finally freak-out everyone when I whip out what looks like a .38-caliber snub-nosed revolver and fire it at Woodrow. The flash, smoke and explosive sound of the gun absolutely terrifies the bastard.

I didn't hurt Woodrow. What I'd actually fired at him was a blank from a harmless starter's pistol—the fake gun you hear at track-and-field events. All the same, I obviously fucked-up Woodrow's nervous system because the next day, while I'm on the phone in a Theater Arts Department office, he walks in with two armed campus security officers and points at me. The campus cops rush me, cuff and search me and drive me to their headquarters, where some guy interrogates me and then turns me over to LAPD cops who take me back to the same jail where I'd spent my Bodega Bay Thanksgiving Sunday.

Only this time they don't put me in the cage with all the other guys. This time they put me in a one-person cell, after which they tell me I'm going to be arraigned on charges of "attempted murder."

Needless to say, I make my one phone call to Elliot and tell him my story; he tells me not to worry and not to talk to the cops. He then, I later learned, calls a big-shot judge he knows and a few minutes after that the cops holding me get a phone call ordering my immediate release. An officer unlocks my cell. He frowns and says, "You must know someone downtown." When I leave the station, Elliot, a little baffled, is waiting in his car. Now I want to shoot Woodrow with my .45 and nuke UCLA. Elliot gets me to forget about violence and help him plan my defense.

Elliot a few days later had me meet with Diana, a staff lawyer in the Los Angeles City Attorney's office (Elliot told me his law firm had done some favors for the city attorney's office). I told Diana my whole story about surrealism and the starter's pistol. She asked me a few questions and concluded the interview with a smile that said "Don't worry." A day or two after that, Elliot told me all charges against me had been dismissed. I was free to return to my doctoral studies.

Which I did. I also, with Elliot's help, took the initial steps toward filing a federal lawsuit against Woodrow and the university for several egregious violations of my civil rights (we later dropped it). Moreover, I continued to disrupt my seminars and continued to make radical speeches to the kids in my discussion group. In time, the entire film-studies faculty and some neocon deans rallied against me and formally expelled me from UCLA.

I think that was my goal. I had driven off my one academic friend, Andrew; I was tired of fighting Woodrow and the other morons: Time to give up on film and school and find something else to do.

# "THE FEW, THE PROUD…"

My first attempt to leave UCLA and Ph.D. work came a few months before my expulsion and was somewhat bizarre. In early 1977, for conscious reasons I don't remember, at a day and time I don't remember, I phoned the main Los Angeles-area recruiting office of the United States Marine Corps—and told a Sergeant Riker I was interested in becoming an officer in the Corps. Sgt. Riker was a superb recruiter (he could get a neo-Nazi to join B'nai B'rith). He answered all of my excited questions with a soft yet exhilarating stream of encouraging, colorful answers, comments, asides and funny metaphors.

In my madness and never-ending search for male role-models, I made an appointment to see him the next day.

The Marine Corps recruiters were in a big armed-forces building squatting on a leafy stretch of Wilshire Boulevard near downtown. Sgt. Riker was the first real Marine I'd ever met. I recall him wearing a khaki shirt with medals and campaign ribbons and dress-blue slacks with a red stripe down each side and a brass belt buckle with the USMC's flag-and-anchor emblem and super-shined black shoes—he looked so military, so cool.

We talked at length about the Corps and my lifelong interest in the military and my college work, especially my thesis on WWII documentaries (I put some sort of credible spin on the Ph.D. debacle in progress) and about my English professor father's having served in military government in Europe during World War II.

When he asked what part of the Corps I wanted, I said that after Quantico (the USMC's Officer Candidates School, or OCS) I was hoping to land a spot in tactical intelligence. I wasn't completely sure I knew what "tactical intelligence" entailed in the Corps, but I thought it sounded like something a Quantico candidate might want to get into.

In the course of all this, we smoked a lot (you could do that in offices back then), and he kept lighting my cigarettes before lighting his own. This deferential act pleased me. In my crazy mind, I thought he was already treating me like an officer.

The sergeant next introduced me to the other recruiters on duty; he did this as if I were already one of the few, the proud. Or so I imagined.

Then he took me to meet the captain in command. This guy was all Marine. Formal. Tough. Courteous. He quietly told me he'd spoken with Sgt. Riker after I'd called the office and said he was happy to have a high-potential applicant like me. I figured this guy's got to like me: The U.S. military was still suffering from Post-Vietnam-Stress-Syndrome—careers in the Corps were a hard sell.

After the captain, Sgt. Riker showed me a terrific Marine combat film, with troops sliding down ropes from helicopters, blasting away with M-16s, chucking grenades, overrunning the enemy. I savored it.

And as I left, the sergeant gave me Marine recruiting posters plus a "The Few. The Proud. The Marines." bumper sticker and a big red-blue-gold flag-and-anchor decal for the rear window of my car. I thanked him, noting I was a big NASCAR (stock car racing) fan and drove a muscle car. He came out to inspect my Challenger and he liked it. I was so proud.

Before my next meeting with the sergeant, I completed an extensive written application for Quantico. I was pleased with my entries, especially those regarding my firearms ownership and use.

But as for the application's question about illegal drug use, shit, I was a '60s Woodstock kid. What I could honestly answer was that from 1966 to 1973, I along with everyone I knew and several million other Americans I didn't know, had variously done grass, hash, acid and speed—along with potent, Native-American hallucinogens.

If I wrote "No illegal drugs, alcohol only," I was sure they'd never believe me, so I entered "Marijuana, briefly as a college undergraduate, experimentation only."

As for psychiatric problems, well, obviously, I had none. Which at that point in time and space I insanely believed.

Happy with my application, I gave it to Sgt. Riker when I next went to headquarters to take an intelligence test, no problem, and a long, detailed psychological test: Here I tried to project a mature young man with normal affect and a strong heterosexual libido—a rock-solid integrity guy whose values and overall personality nicely fit those of a warrior-leader.

o o o

A few day later, the Sergeant called, said my application and test scores looked good, asked me to have my college transcripts sent to him along with letters of reference and told me my physical fitness test would be next: something like 100 sit-ups, 25 pull-ups and running a certain number of miles (I forget exactly how many) in a certain number of minutes. Failing to pass this test disqualifies you from the Corps.

I was 26 and lean but out of shape, so I started training. Sit-ups were no worry; I'd been doing them on and off since sixth grade to neurotically make sure I'd never have a pot belly.

No, my only big worry was the run. I hadn't run anywhere in a decade, and I'd been smoking heavily for years. Upshot: I bought UCLA Bruins running shorts, a UCLA Bruins T-shirt and Puma sneakers. Then I started running a daily course around my neighborhood. Each time I ran, I was faster, less winded. I was determined to be a Marine.

In line with this, I'd ironed onto my shorts a large round Marine Corps emblem the sergeant had given me. And while running, I thought people driving by would see my big emblem and think, "Hey, he's a Marine, he's cool." (Likewise, I thought while I was driving, other drivers were spotting the big round blue-and-red Corps emblem blazing from my rear windshield and think, "Hey, he's a Marine, he's cool.")

I thought things like that.

Especially while driving to meet Sgt. Riker for my test. When I got there, he was in his nifty Marine Corps running outfit and holding a stopwatch. I easily passed the sit-ups. I stalled on the last few pull-ups, but the sergeant wordlessly grabbed my hips and gave me a conspiratorial boost or two. I passed.

Next we go outside for the run—the course is through an old-money neighborhood just south of headquarters and Wilshire Boulevard. L.A.'s weather is perfect: 75 degrees, low-humidity, a slow steady wind off the Pacific. Sgt. Riker grins, hits his stopwatch and quietly says, "Let's do it."

He runs by my side, setting the pace, checking our time. I'm happy to have him there. I keep right up with him, feel terrific. After a minute or so, he starts chanting loudly, something like "I don't know but I've been told Mary won't but her sister will."

I'd heard and enjoyed martial chanting in films, but hearing it in real time is a real high. He tells me to join in and I do, which helps my breathing and makes me feel very Marine-like.

Then he switches to a new verse as we hit our second mile, something like: "I don't know but I've been told all Marines are strong and bold." I chant with him. I'm getting gitty, endorphins kicking in, even more so on the next mile.

He glances at his watch, "We're right on the money," he smiles.

More sidewalk, more trees, more shafts of light. "C'mon," he says, "let's sprint to the finish."

I pass! Bend over, winded, sweat-soaked. He laughs and slaps my back, shouting "Good run, with time to spare!"

o o o

Still, I wasn't in. I had to pass a number of medical exams. Paranoid my imipramine would show up in my urine or blood, I went off it cold-turkey and flushed away what capsules I had left.

A few days later, I'm back at headquarters for the medical. Now this involves a big, cold, semi-dark floor with 26-year-old me and some 300 guys who look 17 and are trying for the enlisted ranks; all of us are stripped to our briefs or boxers and sergeants are herding us in small groups from one nurse or doctor to another for height, weight, vision, hearing, reflexes, hernia and so on. One doc told us to face the wall and spread our "cheeks"—then he peered inside each of us with a flashlight. "What the hell is he looking for?"I laughed to myself.

Overall, I'm thinking the entire medical is hilarious, a surreal circus.

While my group is finally getting dressed, a kid next me, perhaps sensing I don't quite fit in, asks me if I'm going to Camp Pendleton for basic training. I quietly say, "No, Quantico." He looks at me with what I take to be great respect bordering on awe—and I feel so cool, so proud. An officer.

A week or so later, having passed the medical, I am in the Captain's office. He shakes my hand, smiles and congratulates me. Then, with me flanked by Sgt. Riker and three other recruiters, he has me raise my hand and take an oath of loyalty to the Constitution and to the Corps.

That done, he tells me that my acceptance to Quantico is "provisional" because we still need the formal, albeit routine, approval of naval headquarters in San Francisco. All I keep joyously thinking is "I'm in! I'm a Marine! Semper Fi!"

o o o

The psychology of my Marine Corps thing is of interest, as I believe my manic-depressive thinking and behavior at the time, at various levels of consciousness and unconsciousness, brutally interacted with the rest of my psychology: my feeling no genuine self-esteem, no moral, intellectual or physical courage, no real identity; I filled all these gaps—perhaps like other people only exponentially and multidimensionally more so—with the Corps. The Corps would save me in every way, I believed. It would give me a new and precise reason to live. It would give me an entirely new, rock-solid identity. A new self.

o o o

But when Sgt Riker phoned me to set a date for the Captain to brief me on Quantico, he sounded grim, asked me to come in that afternoon. When I get there, he and the Captain look angry. The Captain tells me San Francisco has rejected my application for officer candidates school. He apologizes, saying he was to blame because he'd seen my marijuana comment and thought it honest and to be expected from a young man who'd gone to college in the late '60s—in fact, he didn't think anyone at headquarters "would give a damn."

The three of us commiserate a little, I hide my disbelief and shock. The Captain thanks me at length for all the effort, says he admires me, gently punches my shoulder.

Sgt. Riker walks me to the elevators—where he angrily tells me, "The Captain really fought for you. But they said you didn't have a chance." Sgt. Riker shuts his eyes. "And all because some dick-head admiral up there said he didn't want some 'dope-smoking ex-hippie' in the Corps."

## *"CHARACTERS WELCOME"*

USA Network

With the Marines a no-go in the late spring of 1977, my mania peaked and in super-slow-motion and with great stealth, I sank into a mixed-state that would take me into another major depression.

My descent, nevertheless, took nine months. And until I was down for the eight count, I was living in an alcoholic blackout without the alcohol; I was functional, lucid, productive—and yet shrink-wrapped in a mixed-state of delusion and anomie. A flight controller might say I was vectoring all over the place.

Lucky for me, just before my expulsion from UCLA, I'd registered with its career-placement center for work as a professional freelance writer, editor or English tutor. The job people, who knew nothing about my war with the university, were soon referring me to callers who needed a person with my skills.

My first client turned out to be a mother lode: Phillip Blair and Associates, Consulting Structural and Civil Engineers—a boutique firm with a knack for winning federal contracts to produce esoteric engineering reports. Indeed, my first assignment, for $1,600 (in 1977 dollars), was editing a monster document titled something like "Criteria for the Evaluation of Manufactured-Housing Quality-Assurance Inspection."

Phillip Blair was a bright, kind, soft-spoken guy. He liked me and my work. I liked him. I wrote or edited his reports for the next nine months. And I admired his spending most of his government earnings on his true love which was architectural preservation and restoration (when I first met him, he and his staff were passionately restoring a magnificent but crumbling and abandoned Victorian-era railroad station).

I also had other clients, like Donald, a subliterate USC graduate student from a wealthy family in Orange County. At $15-an-hour, I wrote almost a year's worth of his term papers and take-home exams.

During this period of freelance work, my sex drive, still high, pushed me to plunge into love affairs with numerous women—each relationship, as always, and mostly thanks to me, a disaster.

In time, I gave up on women, gave up on any social life and began to give up on life, spending my free time drinking at home alone, a little more booze each week; I particularly liked the "stopping power" of 94-proof Beefeater gin-and-tonics, their singular ability to kill off my demons, at least for a few hours.

As in past moodswings, I also used food to quell what was clearly the onset of major depression. I then imagined I was getting fat, which only caused me more anxiety, leading, of course, to more eating. And so on.

I was beginning to have an unprecedented rough time writing for Phillip: blocks, confusion, frustration, fear, panic. I several times took to lying on my bed, closing my eyes and pointing my Colt .45 against my heart. And yet I couldn't pull the trigger. I was still ambivalent about death. What's more, the image of a hollow-point blowing up my body was too much. I couldn't do that to myself.

And I was sane enough to realize I had to get psychiatric help. Unable to afford a private shrink, I went to a Los Angeles County health clinic in West Hollywood and ended up talking to a young social worker.

He seemed smart and sensitive, listening to me, better than most shrinks, describe my psychiatric history and present alcoholic-suicidal condition. I cried in front of him. Of course I cried: I'd slipped into delusion, groundless sadness, catastrophic expectations, twisted memories and self-hate. And, common in this condition, I was crying over crying and crying over that.

The social worker ended our session by saying with some urgency he wanted me to return the next day and meet with a psychiatrist. I agreed.

Driving home afterward on Melrose Avenue in the rain, I abruptly turned onto a side street and parked. Then I cried again, heavily, with my head against the steering wheel: I felt the social worker, at least one person in the world, cared about me.

o o o

The county psychiatrist I saw a day later was a Dr. Wolffe, a handsome, furrow-faced man in perhaps his late 50s. He had an energetic, reassuring bedside manner.

I later learned Dr. Wolffe was not a county employee but rather a volunteer: Once weekly, this psychiatrist donated a day of his expensive time (he had a lucrative private practice near world-chic Rodeo Drive in Beverly Hills) and considerable intellect, insight and skill—to the West Hollywood area's small but needy population of people like me.

With him was a small group of white-coated medical students with clipboards who listened closely as he asked me what I realized were exactly the right questions for a shrink to ask a hard-core manic-depressive.

Every so often he underscored to the students something I said; when he was done interviewing me, he turned from me to his students and incisively summed up my condition.

Distressed as I was, I was amazed at how informed and informing Dr. Wolffe was about manic-depression. He had a feel for the illness; he knew it better than anyone I'd ever met by that first week in January 1978.

Moreover, he gave me prescriptions for imipramine, to reverse my depression—and for lithium to prevent an upward swirl into mania. He said he would personally arrange the requisite blood testing and monitor my lithium level to keep it optimal.

No one—not at Carrier, certainly not at Livingston, UCLA or the Los Angeles Free Clinic—no one had ever done this with me before. No one had ever put me on a formal regimen of both drugs at once. In retrospect, it seems so obvious. (True, my old Carrier shrink had once mentioned antidepressant-induced manias, but he never did anything about it.)

Dr. Wolffe's treatment worked. I felt the imipramine kick in about two weeks later and the lithium not long after that. I could have continued my freelance writing but its allure had soured, and I started thinking about how I could earn a steady paycheck as a nonfiction writer on somebody's staff.

Why not a daily newspaper?

# 100 MILES DUE NORTH OF SAN FRANCISCO

I ended up calling 66 daily newspapers, large and small, in California, Nevada and Arizona, asking one city editor after another if he had any openings for a rookie, and if he did, could I send him my resume and copies of my published work and could I come in for an interview?

I found three small-town California papers that had an opening for a freshman reporter. And one of them hired me to cover education and do features for $175 a week. I was elated—and the elation was healthy.

For the next two and a half years, I was a staff writer for the *Ukiah Daily Journal*, an afternoon daily—the only daily newspaper in all of Mendocino County, California—that gave its readers world and national news from a wire service and detailed local coverage from its five reporters and two editors.

Ukiah was not only the Mendocino County seat, but also the vast, rural beautiful county's only "city" (at the time, population 15,000), some 100 miles due north of San Francisco on US. 101.

I had never lived in a rural area. And although I missed L.A. from the moment I left it, I also reveled in what to me was a foreign country, perhaps a cross between Scotland, Ireland and Switzerland.

The first thing I noticed was the air—so cool, clear, clean, no L.A. 24/7 smog-gunk. Then I saw the redwood-carpeted mountains of the Coastal Range hemming the narrow Ukiah Valley, and undulating vineyards and hyper-green, boulder-studded pastures with real sheep. Where am I? This is all such a trip. And I'm on the right meds, I'm in control.

I later discovered Santa Rosa in Sonoma County, an hour's drive south on 101, a road with only two lanes twisting through mountains high above the Russian River. I also discovered that a different two-lane road through the mountains gets me to the Pacific Ocean and the misty, mesmeric beauty of a village named Mendocino, perched above white-capped waves.

o o o

The only writing I'd ever done for a newspaper was film criticism at Livingston. I knew zero about writing news copy, let alone how to research and type out an important story in the course of one morning and get it on the city editor's desk before deadline.

Deadline. What a terror at first. We had the same deadline (was it noon? I forget) every day. I'd never had to write so fast, with virtually no time for rewriting (for me writing until then had always involved extensive rewriting). My first week I handed in a story a few minutes after deadline; the city editor, Mitch, without a word picked up my story and dropped it on the floor. It didn't run. I panicked, sure I'd be fired. I wasn't fired, and I never missed deadline again.

I not only had to learn newspapering but, more important, I had to find a psychiatrist who'd write me prescriptions for lithium, imipramine and Valium—and order lab tests to keep my lithium level optimal. (Lithium is inherently volatile; when a shrink is stupid or gets lazy and doesn't track your level, terrible things can happen, like the mind-body derangement that comes with lithium toxicity.) I lucked out, I found a first-rate shrink in Santa Rosa who truly knew my illness and how to treat it.

He kept my lithium at a perfect level, albeit with the usual side-effects, most of all a visible tremor in both my hands, which, I feared, made me look like a junkie or Parkinson's patient. My publisher saw it and laughingly nicknamed me "shaky," which I detested—and when *Journal* friends asked me about my hands, I said doctors in L.A. had attributed the problem to my years of overdosing on alcohol, tobacco and caffeine. They believed me.

Somewhat ironically, endemic to the kind of daily newspapering I was doing were super-highs and lows that seemed to mimic in fast-motion my manic-depression. I must have had 50 sharp moodswings a day, but that was okay because my meds stopped me from staying too high or too low for too long.

o o o

By the start of my second year on the paper, I felt comfortable with newswriting, and I got better at it. I was covering all sorts of stuff from local education, crime, politics and business to sexual child abuse (yes, we had our share of sickos; they made me look sane). I also got to write personal-opinion columns, film and theater reviews and editorials—I loved doing these pieces because they allowed the suppressed-manic-depressive in me to take strong, often emotional positions on a variety of topics, quite unlike the fairness and objectivity we strived for in hard-news writing. Sometimes readers in letters or phone calls denounced my work, which angered and hurt me; sometimes they praised it, which felt wonderful.

Either way, for me the beauty of my *Journal* years, put simply, was that my name and my words, and with certain pieces my picture, were rolling off the press almost every day. I was getting published almost every day! This was heaven.

Meantime, I often drove south to Santa Rosa on weekend nights. This city of some 60,000 at the time was upbeat, modern, stylish; it had restaurants and discos not to be found in Ukiah. Indeed, Ukiah always struck me as culturally challenged, too white, too conservative, stuck somewhere in the Dark Ages. I loved the natural beauty of Mendocino County, but I never made peace with Ukiah's Rotary-Club-old-boy-network, with the way the whole place seemed to run in slow-motion or no-motion. My only friends were people who worked at the *Journal*; however even with them, thanks to my chronic social-anxiety disorder and pleasing-child behavior (both immune to my meds), I couldn't socialize or relax or laugh without first getting half-drunk.

By contrast, I never mixed booze with writing. I had—and still have—an odd puritanical rule about that. If I wanted to get hammered, I'd only do it when I didn't have to work the next day. And most nights, before I poured my first gin-and-tonic (I allowed myself three pre-bed ones on work nights), I doggedly studied top newspapers like *The Wall Street Journal* and books on journalism; I wanted so badly to be a good newspaper reporter and writer. I wanted my colleagues and readers to love me; I wanted my father to love me, and I always sent him my best clips.

Here's one of them, a personal feature story you might like. For what it's worth, a number of *Journal* readers, mostly parents, praised it by phone or letter. Precisely why I couldn't pinpoint, save they seemed to see it as a love letter to my father. Maybe it is. At the time, I simply felt I had a good, funny, poignant story, and my father and I at the time were on reasonably good terms. (My sister said I only wrote it so I could hit him up for money; she was projecting: I was fully self-supporting during my *Journal* years and, to the best of my recall, never once panhandled him.)

Okay, here's the clip (I think I'm a much better writer now):

*Ukiah Daily Journal*

**Wednesday, February 27, 1980, Ukiah, California**

**WASTE NOT, WANT NOT**

***[Editor's introduction: "Aching for that romantic vacation on a Mexican beach, or that dream condo at Tahoe? How about that cream-colored Mercedes parked in your wildest fantasy? "It only takes money," says the wizard of the check-out line, whose son explains how his father made it from a Depression slum to a Manhattan suburb."]***

**Saving money.**

**It's impossible for some.**

**And a way of life for others.**

**My father is a champion at saving money. While growing up in the slums of Newark, N.J. during the Depression, he learned money was something to be taken very seriously.**

**Twenty years after the Depression, he had a secure, middle-class income. He was married, the father of two children and had a model house in a model suburb.**

**He also had economic view of the universe. Whenever I'd marvel a neighbor's new Cadillac or swimming pool, he'd solemnly, and with envy, remind me. It only takes money."**

**And when he'd buy a new TV set or get new tires for the car, he'd say, "You see, it only takes money."**

**When I told him I wanted to go to Europe he'd say, "Well son, it takes money."**

**His material lust was reserved for items sold in the finest department stores, the ones that advertised in the New Yorker magazine. Whether our family needed a prestige item or not, he'd buy it if the price was right. Once, from Saks Fifth Avenue in New York City, he bought a tiny silver cup with a tiny silver spoon and a tiny silver cover. It was designed to hold saccharine.**

**Having no need for this container, my mother, sister and I asked why he'd purchased it.**

**"It was on sale!" he said delightedly.**

**My father responded to sales like a shark to blood. Gettting 25 percent less than what the "suckers" had paid the week before was the real thrill.**

**Just because the goods in certain sales were a season or a year out of style, or slightly flawed, was no reason not to buy them. "Who's going to notice a crooked seam?" he asked my sister with contempt when she denounced a sweater he'd bought her without warning.**

**Sometimes he'd come home with shirts for me. They were too big, I hated the colors, and my friends were wearing totally different, up-to-date styles. "You'll grow into them, he said above my protests. "Besides, what do your little pisher friends know about shirts?"**

**My father had a cut-rate tailor. Mr. Bernardi was 86 years old and had lost a leg to leukemia. He was confined to a wheelchair, and had given up tailoring some time ago—except for people from the "old neighborhood" like my father. Because Mr. Bernardi wasn't very concerned with money, he only charged token fees, like $2 for $50 worth of alterations. Sometimes my father would**

**take six suits to Mr. Bernardi, reminding me that the old man "had plenty of spare time on his hands and was happy to get the work."**

**One summer, my father won a fellowship to study at Penn State University, and he took the family with him. He returned one afternoon to our rented house and was unusually excited: He'd just seen a poster for a special event that night called a "Nickel-a-Dip Dinner." It was set for a small church in a tiny town about 50 miles from the university. What attracted my father so much wasn't church or the town, the idea of corn, potatoes, carrots, roast beef, Jell-O, pudding, rolls, and cake at five cents per ladle.**

**He couldn't believe he'd get to feed the whole family for less than $5.**

**And off we went. The church basement was jammed with folks buying nickel-dips of string beans and meat loaf and soup. My father loved the whole affair. He chatted with the kind church women running the dinner as my mother picked at her dips.**

**It was sweltering down there. I hated the food. I knew there had to be something wrong with it if it was only five cents a portion.**

**My little sister cried through supper. Then she threw up.**

**Whenever my father did the family grocery shopping, which was at least once or twice a week, he'd always come home with canned fruits and vegetables. What made the cans different from those other shoppers bought is that they were dented. According my father, cans could get dented by falling from a shelf. Since most customers didn't want food from a dented can ("How silly," he said), supermarkets discounted flawed containers by up to 50 percent. When we warned him the cans might have botulism, my father told us the government would never let that happen.**

Even more attractive to my father than bashed-in cans were supermarket "specials." If a supermarket was selling paper towels and a discount price of six rolls for $1, my father would grab 20 rolls. This wasn't greed, and our family had no special need for paper towels. But to my father, buying 30 rolls on sale meant a massive savings over what the "suckers" would be paying once the special ended.

To save money another way, my father made sure our family made do with store-brand products as opposed to the one advertised on TV. He adamantly maintained there was no difference between store-brand goods and brand-name ones except that the latter cost more.

Had visitors wandered into our bathroom or linen closet, they have found Macy's shampoo, Macy's cotton swabs, Macy's cotton balls, Macy's facial tissues, Macy's alcohol, Macy's toothbrushes, Macy's dental floss , Macy's sanitary napkins, and Macy's toilet paper.

My father also bought supermarket-brand wines in huge jugs. He'd serve the wine to guests in fancy decanters and assure me, "They'll never know the difference."

Long before recycling became nouveau-chic, my father was saving money by recycling paper towels. He'd get us to use the same one in the kitchen for three or four days running, laying it out each night to dry by the side of the sink. My father's slogan for this was, "Waste not, want not."

One money-saving technique of his that pre-dates today's energy consciousness was his keeping the heat low and the lights off. He was forever telling to put on sweaters when we complained about the semi-Arctic temperatures he'd subject us to. When we were in pajamas, he never failed to say, "If you don't want to be cold, wear a robe." I'm not giving my money to the gas company" And when we left the front door open too long during winter, he'd yell at us to shut it. "You're letting out the heat!" he'd scream, as if he were losing blood.

He was also determined to frustrate the electric company. If one of us left a room without turning off the lights, he'd be there in a second to turn them off. He rigged the house with timing devices that would turn certain lights on after dark to discourage burglars; this way, we could take a trip without having to leave the lights on 24 hour a day, thus cutting down on the electric bill.

Because of the money involved with air conditioning a big house, my father opted for a much cheaper attic fan. This device is supposed to cool a house by sucking air through it. Unfortunately, summer nights in New Jersey are hot and humid, and our fan sucked hot, humid air through our bedrooms for years, until my father give in and bought air conditioners, which he'd found on sale.

A big baking company in the heart of Newark had a special store where cookies, bread, and donuts were always on sale. My father stopped there once week and bought bag after bag of bakery items for next to nothing. He could do this because the store only sold damaged good. The chocolate-chip cookies were pathetic fragments of what had been whole cookies, crushed or cracked during the baking or packaging process. The donuts had no holes. And the bread was at least day-old or packaged sideways or sliced into twice the normal number of pieces.

"Eat it," he'd say. "There's nothing wrong with it. People just don't like the way it looks."

"Aw. Do we have to?" my sister and I would plead.

"Don't be silly. If you won't, I will," he'd say, biting into a chocolate-chip fragment. """You don't know what you're missing. This isn't deformed. It's good."

Bicycles were a big sore spot between my father and me because I always wanted new ones and he, in the name of saving money, always bought me used ones.

On the way to school one spring, my friends and used to pass an ugly, red, used, three-speed bike chained to lamppost. "For Sale," said the sign on it.

My friends and I called it a "piece of crap."

When my birthday arrived that spring, the "piece of crap" was waiting for me in our garage, compliments of my father.

To this day, my father still collects coupons, returns empty bottles, and uses the back of envelope as scratch pads, his more formal stationery being whatever he lifts from work.

Of course, he doesn't always succeed in saving. Once he tried to save money by using bottom-of-the-line paint on the exterior of our house. In less than six months, the entire house began to peel, and he had to shell out a fortune for repairs and a decent paint job.

He's dauntless nonetheless. Only 59 years-old—and 11 years away mandatory retirement—he recently lied his way into the National Society of Retired Persons. Members of this group, he told me, get discounts nationwide on rental cars, hotel room, and packaged tours.

Which is important for my father because he likes to travel. But unlike most world travelers his age, he doesn't book hotel room in advance. When he and my mother arrive in a foreign city, they spend hours driving to El-Cheapo lodgings listed in books like "Europe on $5 a Day." When my father decides he's found a bargain, the exhausted couple settles in for the night, and makes dinner from groceries picked up earlier.

"Why waste money in restaurants," says my father.

When he does eat out, he tips at the rate of 5 percent. "Why should I have to pay the waiter's salary?" he always asked rhetorically.

He loves the theater in London because it's quite the opposite of Broadway when it comes to ticket prices: The most inexpensive seats in London theaters are in the orchestra. My father' been known to sit through the worst play in all England just to relish the luxury of a $2 orchestra seat. "This would have cost me $25 on Broadway, he'd say to himself as the curtain rose.

Of course he does have his contradictions. When it came to the medical needs of our family, he'd pay every penny the doctor ordered. He'd moan, but he'd pay for the best care available. When my sister or I got into serious financial jams in and after college, he was always there to help. He griped, he always made us feel guilty ("I just to spent $3,000 to have the house reroofed; your mother's car is on its deathbed; the TV is on the blink") and then he helped us out.

Once, after his first moonlighting job as a $100-per-day consultant, he made $500. He was overjoyed; it was the kind of high-income work he'd dreamed of. Then I called long-distance to say I desperately needed $500 for a new transmission. I was living in Los Angeles at the time, mass transit was a mess, and my job demanded a car. He knew that. And, after telling me he felt sick, he sent the money.

**My sister later told me he'd sent me he sent the $500 he'd just earned consulting.**

**"He was heartbroken," she said.**

**That was how it was. When the auto insurance was due and I didn't have the money, he'd bitch and scream, and come through. When I ran out money half-way through a two-month stay in Washington D.C., he gave me $500. When I needed $1,000 to relocate for a new job in a new city, he was there.**

**"What are parents for?' He'd ask.**

**He and I would always call the money a "loan," but that was his way of giving and my way of taking without his feeling angry and me ashamed.**

**He loved to spend money. And he loved to save it. The only way he could do both was to stalk bargains from Safeway to Saks.**

**He drove us crazy. But our family never went broke. And in some tangled way I'll never sort out, he knew what he was doing.**

o o o

By the end of my second year at the *Journal*, spring 1980, I'd had two disastrous love affairs. Despite those failures, however, I did have one very close fellow-reporter friend, one of the finest guys I'd ever met. He and his fiancé left Ukiah shortly after I; he joined the Associated Press and after that the *Los Angeles Times*. Via visits, phone calls, letters and emails, we maintained our friendship for 23 years, until, I'm afraid, he simply couldn't cope with my madness anymore. I don't blame him a bit. Sometimes he shows up in my dreams—in one of them, I see him in the distance walking away from me.

At any rate, I was at this time also applying to much larger newspapers for a job; came close but never landed one. Which was okay because I was now ambivalent toward newspaper journalism: The strict style and content rules of newspaper writing were beginning to bore me; I wanted writing that offered more literary freedom. I'd also begun to miss L.A. terribly and was avidly planning my moving back and getting a writing job in PR (public relations) or advertising—in addition, I wanted to try personal, freelance nonfiction a la Tom Wolfe.

My Ukiah years, nevertheless, rank among the most intense, exciting and productive of my life. To this day, I'm proud of them. And despite some hypomanic crazy moments, I never owned weapons (I'd sold my Colt and Gerber knife while packing for Ukiah), never got arrested, never got a speeding ticket. I actually managed my money carefully: never bounced a check, always paid my bills on time, and, thanks to bankruptcy, never had a credit card to abuse.

# THREE-POINT LANDING

With no new job lined up, I left the *Journal* in June 1980 and in a controlled delirium raced straight down Interstate 5 to L.A.

Being back in L.A. was like returning, with a mix of profound appreciation and love, to a woman I'd once walked out on. I probably would have gone manic had not my meds been working.

For starters, as in Ukiah, I had, sequentially, several flame-out love affairs. That I don't get explicit or lengthy about my love life is simply because, from my reading, conversation and experience, I believe mine has been no different from what a few billion other people have done or are doing as I write this. Although by the mid-I '80s, I was seriously beginning to suspect my illness and psychology made me incapable of having a successful love relationship with a woman. Then again, what was "successful?"

In the early '80s, I also had serious problems with my pre-Ukiah L.A. friends. Time and experience hadn't touched them: They were oddly exactly the same as when I'd moved north in early 1978. But Ukiah had miraculously matured or at least changed me for the better, and I realized I was hanging out with some very sick, toxic people. So in various ways I ejected them from my life for good. I finally decided not to have any human relationships outside of work or my neighborhood bar.

During this same period, I was thinking about, and had been for years, a vasectomy. With encouragement from a lover at the time, I finally in late 1980 went to Planned Parenthood in L.A. and arranged for the surgery. You see, I was now age 30 and since my early teens I've never wanted to legally marry and have the kind of loveless, joyless marriage my parents were mired in—and I've absolutely never wanted to be a father. I knew how self-obsessed, neurotic and love-challenged I was. To be legally and morally responsible for the overall growth, and especially the mental health, of another human being was to me unthinkable, verboten.

That my kid would be manic-depressive or schizophrenic or otherwise seriously fucked-up was a sure bet. And I was certain I'd turbocharge my kid's inherited illness by being no less physically and no less psychologically abusive than my own father. I might even surpass him.

Add to my miswired mental DNA and sick learned behavior my being a functional alcoholic and happily addicted smoker: great role-model for a child, huh. (I've been smoking for exactly 41 years; funny, after giving me a physical exam a few months ago, my doctor said she was amazed at how clear my lungs were; I told her I had strong pulmonary DNA. I didn't tell her I sometimes feel genetically condemned to live.)

Okay, my vasectomy day comes. I'm really happy, finally, I'm doing it! And bang, big trouble. I have a preoperative meeting with the urological surgeon at Planned Parenthood; he tells me he doesn't want to do my vasectomy, thinks I'm too young for it, thinks I might in the future want to marry and want to have children, and the reversal rate for vasectomies isn't exactly terrific. I think he's projecting. I will never ever want children.

So I play the "Sanity Card." I explain and stress as cogently as I can that my genetic gun is loaded, that any child of mine would have a

99.999% chance of developing my madness. I tell him my relative stability on meds could in no way improve my DNA or help me be a good father. (Fact is, I often think people like me should not be allowed to breed—but when I told this to a smart shrink, he asked, "Who is to decide? And by what criteria?")

Anyway, the sanity card worked: The guy gave up, and I eagerly changed into a surgical gown. The resultant operation, under a local anesthetic, took about 20 minutes, with the surgeon cutting into my scrotum, snipping and tying off some conduits, and, quite considerately, telling me at each step what he was doing. (Planned Parenthood people had already taught me in detail about the procedure but hearing the surgeon's narrative was reassuring.)

Result: My sperm cells would not enter my semen; they would die and my body would absorb them. I was medically sterile, or as they say, I'd be "shooting blanks." Today, 28 years later, and numerous sperm tests and many lovers and no pregnancies, my vasectomy is still working perfectly. Semper Fi!

I was extremely pleased with my surgically induced infertility. But nothing about my getting it was unique: Millions of other men had done it or were planning to; perhaps the only difference is that they were older than I and made their decision only after they'd fathered a number of children and with their wives had decided they didn't want any more. I didn't care about my age or unmarried status: I knew what I was doing. No way was I going to replicate my madness.

From my vasectomy in 1980 onward, I stayed stuck, despite good meds, in my neurotic manic-depressive psychology plus my nonstop father-transference, nonstop projection and nonstop pleasing-rebellious child behavior.

With all this shit I doomed the raft of subsequent love affairs I've noted, which ran from living together for three years to one-night stands to assorted short-term stuff.

I also took my psycho-garbage into a full-time staff-writing job I landed in 1980 at Orthopaedic Hospital, a major, nonprofit, specialty-medical center in downtown L.A. that treated people with myriad bone, muscle, tissue and nerve disorders and related psychosocial problems.

For the hospital's well-financed public-relations department, I was the senior writer for the next five years, producing a quarterly magazine for old-money donors, a monthly employee newspaper, marketing pieces, patient-education booklets, an annual report, press releases and various kinds of copy for other departments and for stellar doctors who couldn't write their name. During these years, I never once mentioned my illness or meds for fear, paranoid I don't know, I'd be fired, lose my apartment, end up on skid row.

For the first time in my professional life, I had my own office and a steadily increasing salary. As in Ukiah, I also had good health and vacation benefits and for the most part awfully good people to work with. I wore cowboy boots, snap-down western shirts and cords to work every day, no one cared, this was a very tolerant place.

Clearly, I'd found my perfect professional home. And yet I was ambivalent toward my job almost from the start, in fact I had a five-year love-hate affair with it. Sometimes I'd secretly apply for openings elsewhere, sometimes I thought I'd stay at Orthopaedic for life. A shrink once told me I was ambivalent about everything. Whatever: Despite my meds and weekly group therapy, I was either an arrogant, abrasive, rebellious employee, or a puerile sycophant.

No wonder I drove straight to my bar after work.

Don't get me wrong, I truly enjoyed my writing and worked doggedly at it; no, my problem, as always, was with a few of my hospital superiors who, I felt, were mistreating or exploiting me—people I turned into bad-fathers whom I at once feared and hated.

I was lucky. They seemed to sense I was crazy—some of them certainly were—but they kept me on because they valued my work and to get it were willing to tolerate my less-than-darling personality.

# DRIVEN AND DRIVING

During my Orthopaedic years, I every morning, while driving some ten miles from my West Hollywood apartment to the hospital, for a few minutes broke through my meds, thought the Santa Monica Freeway was Daytona International Speedway, tore out of the long on-ramp as if I were coming out of the pits, crossed six crowded lanes of traffic in one nonstop diagonal move and, hoping to scare or impress other drivers (very sick) ripped past them at bursts of 85 mph or more. I was in my 30s and still an arrested-disturbed adolescent trying to prove how cool and manly I was. I didn't do this on the surface streets leading to and from the freeway, but once I hit that entrance ramp, I snapped. Once off the freeway, I was simply one more docile, L.A. morning commuter obeying all the traffic laws. That I never in those five years of momentary madness caused an accident or got a ticket to this day amazes me.

o o o

And despite meds which otherwise worked fine, I lapsed into the same idiot driving from 1986 to 1988—only worse—when I was commuting to a different job way out in the San Fernando Valley by way of the Ventura Freeway. To reach my on-ramp from West Hollywood, I had to travel a number of steep and winding two-lane miles through Laurel Canyon.

The moment I fired up the Challenger's 383 cubic-inch engine in my apartment building's underground garage, I crazily thought I was some kind of race-car driver or who knows what. Certainly my car was a Freudian penis symbol, but more important it was me and I was it: I mentally merged with its engine, sheet metal, spark plugs and carb—with its eight headers and two grumbling exhaust pipes.

Laurel Canyon was usually empty when I hit it, well before the absurd jammed-up morning rush. And every time I entered it, no matter how much I urged myself to drive sanely, I hit it as fast and aggressively as I could, turning the dense foliage and rock—and quiet—of the canyon into my private speedway.

Once in a while, I actually encountered some other maniac in a muscle car and we suicidally raced each other to the canyon's summit, at that point slowing down because we both knew cops liked to hide up there with radar guns.

Then I was on the Ventura Freeway, where for some reason I automatically decided to obey the law, and when I hit my surface street, I lit a cigarette and felt the exhilaration of having made it to work again without killing myself or someone else.

This sick-driving behavior exemplifies what I mean when I talk about my illness and my disturbed psychology still "in place," meds and psychotherapy notwithstanding.

o o o

In line with manic-depression, and on top of its manifestation in my driving, drinking and promiscuity, along with my various neuroses, I also during the 1980s had a spasmodic, fevered affair with casino gambling. With or without whatever woman I was involved with at the time, I loved spending weekends or longer in Las Vegas playing blackjack or jousting with a big-payoff slot machine until broke or exhausted. I rarely left Vegas a winner, but I didn't care. You see, the dramatic, nonstop highs and lows of casino gambling, I now realize, mimicked my manic-depression. And the timelessness of a casino, the glitzy decor, the slot-machines ringing and spitting out coins, the shouting craps players, the stream of alcohol, served to you while you're gambling by pretty, smiling half-naked waitresses—all this sent me into quiet, well-behaved, medicated euphoria.

For lack of money and later a revived addiction to writing, I didn't gamble from 1988 until the mid-1990s when I was living in Fresno (midway between L.A. and San Francisco) and discovered the legal casinos on nearby Native-American reservations.

My meds were working well at the time but my drinking had grown heavier and it occasionally sparked brief manic episodes, which sometimes led to self-destructive gambling; I once in 2003 in one night of blackjack lost $4,000—cash I'd drunkenly borrowed off credit cards via ATMs. That sort of mini-mania in 1996 and again in 2003 pushed me into filing for my second and third bankruptcies.

I no longer go to casinos. I call myself a "recovering-addicted gambler." Thanks to my meds and what sanity I still have, I no longer think about blackjack tables and slots in Las Vegas or on Native-American reservations.

This feels good.

# IT GAVE YOU A RAINCHECK ON LIFE

Okay, let me go back to circa 1980-1981 because during these two years, I'm in my early 30s, I'm living in L.A., which I love dearly and which easily accommodates, almost nurtures, crazy people like me, I'm doing well at Orthopaedic Hospital, writing good stuff, winning praise, making enough money to even save some for the first time in my life, interacting daily and with some success with all kinds of O.H. employees, patients, nurses, doctors and administrators—at the same time, my social life outside the hospital and my love life are Hiroshima after the bomb. Either I have walked out on or driven off all my L.A. friends and lovers. My only remaining friends—from Ukiah and Nantucket—are in New York and D.C. I'm taking some grim satisfaction in being a loner. I'm spending every night alone at home reading, watching PBS and drinking myself to sleep. A bright shrink once told me that by nature we are all "social beings." And I heard another say that by nature we are all "sexual beings." I was neither.

o o o

My self-isolation lasted until the start of 1982, when I decided to live in a bar, that is, to spend all my free time in the Raincheck, at the time a popular neighborhood bar just off the intersection of Santa Monica Boulevard and Sweetzer Avenue in West Hollywood. I was living in West Hollywood, which at the time was unincorporated Los Angeles County surrounded by the city of Los Angeles. (The district later became an independent city.)

The Raincheck was a ten-minute walk from my apartment. On a typical weekend night, the place is dark, smoke-filled and wall-to-wall with customers, all drunk or getting there, most exclaiming this and that, shooting pool, playing the juke nonstop.

This is true: For the next two years, I spend every night after work and every weekend night at the Raincheck: I am a "regular," a functional alcoholic surrounded by fellow regulars who tend to be interesting, intelligent, low-level industry people (or industry hopefuls). They are my "enablers": people whose heavy drinking encourages and validates my own.

I had countless "bar friends," but I kept our relationships inside the bar and could only sustain and enjoy these by staying drunk. Given my painful interpersonal track record, the last thing I wanted was a sober, conventional relationship of any kind with anyone. My success rate at social evasion was 100% until the end of 1983.

Meantime, throughout both years, the medicated part of me fought to control my boozing at the Raincheck. From Sunday night to Thursday night, with another work day ahead and my wanting to wake up with a clear head for writing, I put five pennies on the bar. With each fresh drink, I moved one penny from my left to right. When all five were on my right, no matter whom I was talking with, and I was always talking with someone, I excused myself, left a big tip and went home. On Friday and Saturday nights, I went insane, drinking gin-and-tonics steadily from 8 p.m. to the law-mandated closing at 2 a.m. And if that wasn't enough, I'd go to an illegal "after-hours" bar in a drab, murky room behind an anonymous door on a dark street above Hollywood Boulevard.

Remember: Manic-depressives like me, and I'm not alone, love their alcohol-induced highs, which are like brief mini-manias. These people ride out their massive hangovers. And when sober sooner or later resume drinking.

o o o

I stupidly broke my rule against out-of-bar relationships by getting romantically and sexually involved at the end of 1983 with a Raincheck regular, Katherine, an exceptionally bright woman with a Master's in art history who built models (houses, vehicles, space capsules, anything) for films. We got to know each other at the Raincheck while drinking there. She was on the rebound from a Raincheck guy who'd dropped her for another woman; and I, after two years alone, was ready to try again. Problem was, I was DUI when I decided to get involved with her and I stayed that way during much of the three subsequent, mostly loveless, joyless years we shared an apartment less than a block from the Raincheck.

In the end, her chronic neuroses and mine could no longer coexist. Before I could leave her, she called it quits. And I, like a newly freed slave, joyously packed my Challenger and moved to a new apartment in a yuppie singles building a few blocks away. This was 1986, I was alone again, free at last, and quite happy.

o o o

The year before Katherine and I ended, 1985, was the year I left Orthopaedic Hospital to become "Communications Program Director" at Summit Health Ltd., at the time a fast-paced, fast-growing, profit-driven hospital chain based in Century City, the vast, high-rise corporate scrotum of Los Angeles. I joined Summit Health thinking I'd enjoy the heady, super-expanding world of for-profit healthcare (funny, these capitalists were the kind of people I wanted to nuke when I was in SDS).

But as things turned out, my title was a joke. I directed nothing and the company was communications-challenged. Fact is, I was the CEO's personal speechwriter and all-around wordsmith.

I did a lot of good writing at Summit and after a few months was beginning to feel comfortable there until the malignant narcissist CEO I reported to—a guy with whom I behaved like a little boy trying to please his Nazi father, trying to win his father's love, terrified his father will punish him—until this guy, and some other asshole executives pushed me overboard. Once again, hell was other people. I fell as close to depression as you can get on meds and finally quit cold in 1986. I had no new job lined up, but eventually found one.

# "IN ADVERTISING WE TURN HALF-TRUTHS INTO WHOLE LIES"

Anonymous

I joined Ad Group (Invitational Promotions Inc. Advertising Group) in the summer of 1986 as a staff copywriter. The shop specialized in financial-product direct-mail campaigns for credit unions all over the country.

I loved the work. Unlike journalism and PR, you could push what creativity you had in all kinds of clever, zany directions. Although I had no training in ad copy, I studied it the way I'd taught myself newspaper writing in Ukiah. Time and again, my creative director, colleagues and, most important, our clients, liked my stuff. The writing was challenging, fun, rewarding. I'd sometimes get so revved up over a campaign I'd drive to our empty office on weekends to keep working.

As with my early Orthopaedic Hospital period, I had no friends and no lovers during my two years at the agency. My only socializing was with other Ad Group writers, graphic designers and account executives, and I mostly kept it confined to our workplace. And, as with the hospital and Summit Health, I ate 99% of my lunches in a coffee shop alone in a booth.

As in the past as well, my only egregious problem on the job was other people, especially the fat, delusional-Stalinist-psycho-fuckhead—for me, also, a Satanic father-figure—who owned the agency's parent company and really believed and behaved as if he knew all about advertising. He knew nothing about advertising, and his managerial and social skills on a scale of 1 to 10 were -50.

I hated the sucker. Most everyone at Advertising Group hated the sucker. At the start of my third year there, this jerk decided Ad Group wasn't profitable enough so he closed us; I got laid off.

Which was okay because I'd been thinking about quitting for some time, and, covertly, I'd been writing ad copy for a nearby magazine-publishing company. Moreover, getting laid-off qualified me for unemployment benefits. And most important, because my meds were working quite well, I didn't panic or plunge into major depression.

# THESE GUYS WERE HIGH-ROLLERS

After my 1988 layoff, the magazine company kept giving me more work to do on a freelance basis. And, best of all, without going into detail as to how and why, what was then BKLA (Bank of Los Angeles), based a mile from my apartment in West Hollywood, hired me freelance to write its annual report. After I successfully finished that assignment, the bank for the next two years handed me one lucrative job after another (I billed at $30/hour in 1988 dollars; my annualized gross income was around $60,000—all of which I blew, despite meds). My work ran from press releases, print ads and shareholder communications to the next year's annual report, for which I billed and was paid $6,000, for me a fucking fortune.

Notwithstanding my multidimensional neuroses, all of which were active, I was, as they say, on a roll.

In addition to giving my income a sharp upward spike, BKLA and banking in general excited me. I loved being on the inside of raw capitalism. And unlike past jobs, my father-transference with the executives I wrote for was positive; I liked and respected them, they were nice, bright people; they were good to me and made me feel adult and professional.

And they mentored me about banker stuff like financial "risk," which they discussed in somber tones, especially when they "took a hit" on a big loan gone bad. I also learned about the intricacies of their selling BKLA shares on Wall Street.

(I soon had a crush on Wall Street. Its alternating highs, lows and mixed-states mirrored, for me at least, the dramatic moodswings of alcohol, gambling and most of all, manic-depression—with the Federal Reserve and other market forces acting like lithium to stop the Street and our nation's economy from soaring too high; and like imipramine to keep it from sinking too low.)

In my mind, BKLA's bankers were like Vegas high-rollers, betting big money in a never-ending drive for maximal profit; and they were doing so with an almost mystical mix of financial acumen and pure gut hunch.

To top things off, I won and cherished their praise for my writing. When one of my press releases sparked stories (albeit tiny) the same day in *The Wall Street Journal*, *The New York Times* and the *Los Angeles Times*, the bankers thanked me—and I thought, "Wow, I'm big time!"

o o o

My love life. Let's go back a little. Sometime in early 1988, Ad Group hired a new account executive (in advertising, these people find, service and hopefully retain clients). The new executive was a tall, slender, foxy natural blonde named Eva Raines, age 39 (I was 38). I soon discovered she was quick, sharp, very intelligent, gregarious—she had a terrific feel for marketing and was soon doing well; and with her personality, especially her basic kindness and hysterical sense of humor, she won without trying the praise and affection of everyone at Ad Group, even the fuckhead owner.

(A revealing aside: Eva had no parallel when it came to girl-talk; I one day overheard her telling other agency women how to pleasure themselves by placing Ben Wa Balls in their vagina and then sitting on top of a spinning washing machine.)

Account executives act as the liaison between their agency's clients and their agency's copywriters, graphic designers and senior managers. Eva and I worked on numerous projects together. She was extremely good at what she did. I enjoyed working with her. We made a good team. More important, I guess, is that Eva, along with her endless legs, had riveting aquamarine eyes and a supernova smile: I was and still am love-impaired, but I didn't know this then, and I fell in love with her.

I finally told her so, and I assume she was attracted to me because we soon spent our first night together and then started our work mornings by making-out in the agency's conference room before the others showed up.

We were a couple. And this time, after so many failures with women, I promised myself I'd make this one work. I so badly wanted to prove I could give and accept love the way I thought normal people did.

o o o

Eva and I, as they say, had much in common. We both loved movies, books, cats, NASCAR races, feeding birds, CNN-PBS-CSPAN, class restaurants, no-class restaurants, Haagen-Dazs, holding hands while walking around West Hollywood, Native-American history, casino gambling and more. We had a lot of good sex, fun sex—her friends once called us "rabbits." We loved vacationing: Carmel, the Bahamas, Palm Springs. And no matter how middle-class-conventional our lives, we still considered ourselves '60s rebels—Eva had actually been at Woodstock.

On the professional side, Eva and I during our first three years together were taking in (and spending) a lot of money. I was freelancing for BLKA and other clients, and she, with her sterling feel for marketing moved from executive positions at one company after another until joining a nationwide hospital chain as a marketing vice president.

I say all this because I was proud of her, I loved her drive and talent. And her will to live: Some 20 years earlier she'd almost died from Crohn's disease, an especially hideous intestinal disorder; three major surgeries pushed it into remission but the docs had to take out a good chunk of her intestine; worse still, the disease could return. She lived with this, and perhaps her sharp sense of mortality led her to take a singular pleasure in simply being alive.

o o o

Our relationship on every level and in every way grew better and better between 1988 and 1992. She knew everything about my illness and accepted it, and I was remarkably stable and productive, albeit highly neurotic. In late 1992 we left L.A. and settled into a plush apartment in the rich part of Fresno, the city, as I mentioned earlier, midway between L.A. and San Francisco (in California's gargantuan Central Valley).

o o o

This is a long, absurd story so I'll simply say that a few months before we moved, the Los Angeles County Department of Mental Health was bent on recouping the monstrous amount of money I owed it for 12 years of meds, and for five years, 1980-1985, of its group therapy, which it made me attend weekly because I was getting the meds.

I hated every nanosecond of the county's therapy group. The two social workers who ran it said practically nothing of any value during all my time with them; instead, they sat mostly in silence every session while for 90 intolerable minutes the other patients and I (whom the county absurdly called "clients," as if we were sane and involved in some kind of business) whined about the same problems week after week. I was so happy when the two social workers finally transferred to other positions and the fucking group folded.

All the same, I had to see a county psychiatrist monthly from 1980 to 1987 to get my medication prescriptions. These guys were real washouts from their field; I saw various ones over the years, and with the exception of one, they were the worst, most incompetent, fucking-total-jerk-off malpractioner shrinks I'd ever dealt with. I should have reported one of these quacks to the medical board for refusing for more than a year to put me back on Valium or any other sleeping aid, and consequently causing me a lot of insomnia; this same cretin spent most our sessions talking about the poetry he'd written (and asking me to read it), about his vacation cruises, and about his playing some Asian musical instrument I don't remember. I stupidly decided not protest but instead to be a pleasing child, nod "yes" to whatever nonsense he spurted, get my damn prescriptions and get out. Again, father-figure transference. I felt he had all the power, I felt trapped, I hated his guts and wanted to punch him out.

Lady Luck intervened. I one day showed up for my theater-of-the-absurd monthly appointment with this asshole and was told he'd been transferred to another facility. "Halleluiah!" I silently shouted.

As for my prescriptions (we called them "scrips"), I was told to join the county's "medication group." This was terrific: I once monthly sat at a big table in a big room with about 30 other sickos, and when a shrink-assistant of some sort called out our names, we simply walked up to the head of the table and a county psychiatrist silently wrote out our scrips, gave them to his assistant who then handed them to us. I was usually in and out in 15 minutes, making my next five years with the county quite bearable.

That is, until, 1992, my 12th year with the county. You see, since I was always getting some kind of paycheck during these years, I was supposed to be paying for my group therapy, shrinks and med group. Rebellious, furious, indignant-child me thought the county's psychiatric services were so putrid, the damn county should have been paying me to be a "client," who, like the others, helped justify and buttress the existence of the mental health department.

In turn, I never once paid them for anything. Sometimes I agreed to pay, but always found ways not to—and their billing office seems to have lost track of me for years at a time.

Until some young, hot-shot financial administrator one day called me into his office at the start of 1992 (I was 42 by then)—a time when for one reason or another my freelance work had dried up and for once I really couldn't pay the county anything. Didn't matter to this guy, he was determined to get money from me.

Eva at the time was the marketing vice-president for an L.A. medical group and was supporting both of us. I meantime interviewed for and didn't get one corporate job after another. Reason: I tacitly communicated to my interviewers that I really didn't want their job, not after immensely enjoying my prior three years of self-employment—the rewarding assignments, the freedom from Nazi employers, the big bucks.

So anyway, I tell the administrator why I can't cough up the payments he's after; he appears to believe me, but then insists I immediately apply for Medi-Cal, California's medical-assistance program for the indigent, and, far more important for U.S. Social Security psychiatric disability benefits (which included Medicare). His reasoning was that once I was on these programs, the county could bill the state and federal governments for what it was giving me; and thanks to the big, monthly Social Security disability payments I'd be getting, I'd be able to pay whatever Medicare and Medi-Cal didn't cover.

Sounded great to me. I applied.

I got both. First the state aid, and then, after considering my case for six months, the feds declared me officially inane. Starting in 1993, they have sent me a monthly disability-benefit check for what is presently, after upward adjustments for inflation, $12, 340.

This money, and ongoing financial help from my father, have made for my total income from 1993 right up to the present. And this income, though hard for reckless-spending me to live on (remember, even mediated manics have a hard time handling money wisely), has thus far enabled me to write full-time without an employer or client. This is heaven.

All the same, I detest living off the feds and my father. I was entirely self-supporting from 1972 to 1990, and I plan to be so again.

o o o

Okay, now that you know about my Social Security, let's get back to Eva and me: We moved to Fresno because Eva's hospital chain needed her to VP marketing at the enormous, top-tier medical center it owned there. She was an instant star on the job and was making big money. I got some freelance work, but not enough to pay my half of our bills, so I repeatedly tried and failed to land a fulltime writing job in advertising. In time, I stopped looking for work and began what became a decade of writing personal columns (op-ed pieces) for local and regional newspapers. Most of my columns made print, but no pay, just a byline, bio note and sometimes a photo. I kept thinking one of the editors who praised and published my pieces would surely one day offer me a staff job—on occasion I flat-out asked for one: The answer I usually got was that they'd love to have me on board but simply didn't have the "budget" for another full-time writer. Fuck them. Seven years into this period, I hit the top of my game when *The New York Times* ran three of my columns between 2000 and 2003. Then I suddenly got sick of providing free copy to newspapers and spent several months writing my memoir about growing up in the '60s (an already oversubscribed topic). I tried hard, but failed, to get a literary agent or publisher. And now I know why: The book was arrogant, disjointed, blurred, plain bad.

o o o

Okay, let's go back to Fresno 1994-1996. Eva and I are visibly and invisibly unraveling. Eva was still Eva, but I was drifting out of her gravitational pull into paranoid self-obsession, sporadic manic episodes and alcoholism. ("You don't fall asleep," she once told me, "you pass out.") Worse still is that I made my writing far more important than her and our relationship, and in tandem defaulted to my loveless, joyless, helpless-little-boy self. My madness despite meds was fighting for center stage. The rest is fairly common: We steadily talked less to each other, did less together, stopped buying each other presents, stopped making love. In time we were merely coexisting in sadly separate orbits. And despite all my years of psychotherapy and self-awareness, I was remarkably oblivious to this.

Eva tried to warn me, perhaps in her own way plead with me, but I was gone. In 1996, not long after my second bankruptcy, Eva wisely decided to save herself from my madness and abruptly called us off. She'd already (without my knowing) bought herself a gorgeous townhouse in Clovis, a fairly prosperous suburb adjoining Fresno, and at the same time found a one-bedroom apartment for me in a sedate complex filled mostly with retired people. She also paid my first six-month's rent in advance.

I had long expected, perhaps wanted, Eva to leave me; thus her ending us was fine with me. The problem was we couldn't fully detach from each other. The place Eva got me, the place I happily accepted immediately, was only three blocks from her townhouse. And for the next two years, we had a close, active, odd, asexual friendship; we acted as if we'd never lived together.

This weird post-breakup behavior ended when I swirled into a mixed-state so bad Eva finally asked me to get the fuck out of her life for good.

I did. And I think I welcomed it, took some grim sick pride in knowing I'd forced the finest woman I'd ever known to eject me from her solar system. Perfect confirmation of negative self-image.

o o o

Eva died in 2000. She was 51. No one seemed to know precisely what happened save that she succumbed to simultaneous kidney and liver failure. Her death leveled me. I wept as I'd never done before and haven't done since. And now, so long after her funeral, she remains vividly alive in me, while I periodically ponder why I destroyed us.

Maybe part of the answer is here: My sister knew Eva and once in private asked her why she and I had failed. Eva answered, "I wanted a man, and I got a son."

Eva and I lasted eight years as a couple, the longest run I've ever had with a woman. With the exception of one, short, drunken dismal affair, I've been alone for the past 16 years. Eva had been my lover, best-friend, mentor, shrink and much more. Problem was, I'm afraid, I unconsciously viewed her as the loving mother I'd always wanted. In addition, I deemed her the only person I needed in my life. She was the only woman I ever thought of marrying (she didn't want kids either).

These days, I fear I'll never again have a woman so close to me. Although I'm often not sure I ever again want anyone so close to me.

# ON THE ROCKS

During and after Eva, roughly 1997-1998, my private psychiatrist at the time kept warning me, doggedly, about my drinking, saying I was killing millions of my brain cells, doing incredible damage to my body and to my life overall.

After several months of his warnings and too many wicked hangovers—meds and alcohol do not mix—I finally stopped drinking and joined a nearby chapter of AA (Alcoholics Anonymous).

I did two separate tours of duty in AA, exactly 90 days each (you learn to count days of sobriety in AA, and your chapter gives you a little plastic trinket to celebrate benchmarks like 30 days without booze, 60 days and so on). This is what I discovered about AA: It is a dime-store religion masquerading as a treatment program for alcoholics. This is my empirically grounded opinion; they can sue me if they want.

Moving on: I was astounded to learn that AA refuses to recognize alcoholism as a symptom of far deeper psychological and psychiatric problems. True, booze-addiction generates a subset of new psychosocial problems—but it remains a symptom. The people I sat with through those long, boring, nightly meetings that never changed in basic form or content from one to the next, where you're in a room with a bunch of "recovering" drunks talking only about their drinking and related fuck-ups—those people, including me of course, had core personality disorders that were clearly at work with or without alcohol.

Which is why, I was told more than once by veteran members, most AA people sooner or later resume drinking.

At the end of each meeting, we would stand, hold hands and mumble some stupid prayer. I rushed straight home to Gatorade and turkey; other members often went out in small groups for coffee at Denny's; they would ask me to join them, and I always had a reason not to. I was immensely happy when in time they stopped asking.

After I quit AA the first time, I plunged into heavy alcohol and eventually rejoined my chapter. The second time I quit AA was for good. Never went back, never will. You see, I realized I wanted to drink.

# WASTED AT RUBY'S

I'd begun to disintegrate before Eva died, but I managed to resume my column-writing and publishing for another two years, still hoping one of my editors would finally hire me. Fat chance.

My mother, meanwhile, died in 2001, leaving my father, as they say, devastated. Here's a newspaper column I published about him and her death:

***The Fresno Bee***
**Saturday, March 9, 2002, Valley Voices:**
***'SITTING SHIVA' EASES THE PAIN OF GREAT LOSS***

**Our father cried during the funeral.**

**And afterward, tears lined his face while he hugged many of the mourners. Before the ceremony last January, my sister and I joined him at the funeral home for a private viewing of his wife and our mother. We were pleased, if not amazed, to see her all but restored to her natural beauty.**

**The only problem for my sister and me was that our mother's coffin wasn't gleaming mahogany or the like, but a Spartan box made of raw pine**

**On asking our father about this, he said that although our branch of Judaism is very different from the Orthodox one, he liked the Orthodox reason for using a pine coffin: It degraded in**

**the soil much faster than traditional hardwoods, allowing the body to quickly merge with nature and the soul with God.**

**Before the pine box and the funeral, our father spent at least four hours daily in my mother's hospital room where, for six weeks she lay unconscious, the unknowing victim of a massive stroke.**

**Our parents had been married 54 years, and to my 81-year-old father, losing the 77-year-old wife he loved was unthinkable. He initially prayed she'd recover, even partially.**

**"I don't care if she's an invalid in a wheelchair," he said. "I want her alive and with me. I can't lose her."**

**Throughout his watch over her, he cried often, and used tender tactics to stop her leaving.**

**He would gaze at her eyes even though they'd been closed since the stroke. He would talk to her even though she couldn't hear him. He would stroke her hair and kiss her face even though she couldn't feel him.**

**After the funeral, some 200 mourners drove to what was now my father's large condominium in Chatham, N.J., a quiet, attractive suburb of New York City a few miles from the cemetery.**

**While most of the mourners were Jews who viewed death as a joining of the soul with God, they also believed that as survivors, they had a traditional duty to "sit *shiva*"—to visit for up to seven days a surviving family and to ease their grief, trying, at least, to begin the transition of the bereaved from the death of their loved one to the life they would now have to face without that person.**

**So the people who quietly crowded our father's home were there to sit *shiva*—a ritual without alcohol or music, but instead a gentle din of hushed conversation.**

**Among the wall-to-wall people were relatives, friends, neighbors and colleagues. Even after several hours passed, none of them left. And more arrived.**

**Meantime, some mourners volunteered to deploy all the donated food and all the treats inside giant gift baskets delivered by messengers.**

**One especially regal basket came from nearby Kean University, where our father has been an English professor for 42 years and is still teaching part-time.**

**In addition to food, the *shiva* featured our family's rabbi, who led the mourners in a poignant prayer for the dead and for our mother.**

**The *shiva* also made our father the person everyone was seeking out. In fact, he'd no sooner start talking to one person or couple or group than other people would come up and hug him and express their sorrow and offer to help him in any way they could.**

**"Thank you," he would say, sadly and sincerely, holding a mourner's hand or arm. "And thank you so much for coming."**

**By the time my father's three days of *shiva* ended, the cascade of warmth and support embracing him had visibly lifted his spirits.**

**Still, when the last mourner had left and the volunteer clean-up crew had returned his home to normal, he felt profoundly alone; he felt the vast, inviolate absence of his lifetime partner, lover and best friend.**

**That night, he once more found sleep impossible; he felt a piercing pain whenever he looked at the empty side of the bed that had always been hers.**

**So he went to the kitchen and, though hardly a drinker, had a few shots of the premium Scotch he normally reserved for guests; now he hoped it would hurry the sleep he caved.**

**Then he went back to bed.**

**Where he cried, softly.**

o o o

My father's loss and my witnessing it seem to have genuinely moved me. Perhaps, I was projecting onto him my own conscious and repressed sadness over losing my mother. As I said, she and I in the year bore before her death were finally getting to know and understand each other.

o o o

In mid-2003, I gave up my job fantasy and stopped writing. I was still on meds but had drifted into a severe alcoholic mixed-state. I wasn't for some reason seeing my regular shrink or any psychiatrist; some primary-care physician was managing my meds, quite badly, especially the lithium: I think I knew this but didn't care. Very dumb. For all practical purposes, when not at home, I lived in a place named Ruby's. It was a quiet, nondescript neighborhood bar an eight-minute walk from my apartment. Most of its regulars were clearly not Raincheck material: Most were either blue-collar people with middle-class incomes and lifestyles or similar people only retired; they were, well, bland. Few said anything worth listening to. And some were outright stupid. But since everyone was drunk, I felt great, surrounded everyday by enablers.

Infused with gin or whiskey or both, I got to know countless people at Ruby's; although, in sober retrospect, I got to know no one. Unlike

Raincheck people, the drinkers at Ruby's were taciturn, even secretive about themselves. Although once in a while I'd get a "talker," some blitzoed whackjob who'd tell me his tragic life story even though I'd never asked to hear his tragic life story. I told no one at Ruby's my life story; no matter how wasted, the only truth about myself I ever revealed to anyone was highly sanitized and wouldn't fill a shot glass.

These were not healthy years for me. I normally drank myself into a blackout every night, waking up late the next day, badly hungover and with zero recall of what I'd said or done at Ruby's after my sixth drink or what I did after Ruby's or how l got home and to bed. Hence the term "blackout": Getting hammered shuts down the surveillance camera in your brain.

My two-year stint at Ruby's ended suddenly one night thanks to a new bartender, who was a man; I note this because all the other bartenders were kind women who mothered me, which I loved, whereas this jerk had been a Ruby's regular and was also the virulently jealous husband of a bright, attractive young woman who liked to sit next to me at the bar and talk about writing (she'd read my columns). Anyway, this jerk husband of hers thought I was hitting on her, or she was hitting on me, or who knows what the fuck he imaged. Whatever his sick case, he one night falsely accused me of abusing the bar's free mini-buffet and pushed me out the front door.

I would've killed the sucker but I was too drunk to kill anybody, and yet, oddly, I went to a nearby pay phone, made a 9-1-1 call to the CPD (the Clovis Police Department—good tough cops you don't mess with) and told them I was going to kill him. They rolled up in seconds (their response time is incredible). I, visibly drunk, told them my story; they went inside and heard the jerk's story; they came outside and told me to go home.

I did, and, out of fury and hurt, never again went to Ruby's. Since then, save for a few brief manic episodes, I haven't been in a bar. Since then, after my day's writing, I've done my drinking alone at home at night. Most always into a blackout.

I repeat: My meds don't kill all the demons. Alcohol does.

# "SHOOT ME, PLEASE SHOOT ME!"

This next period, circa mid-2004 to mid-2006, is a blurred nightmare. Here my memory falters. My lithium level was bouncing all over the place: I'd be walking—sober—on the sidewalk and fall down, I sometimes hallucinated, I punched holes in the walls of my apartment. I took a huge overdose of Dalmane, a sleeping pill, with a mass of alcohol in a frenzied effort to die, but somehow didn't. (A shrink later told me that 30 years of meds had made me "drug-resistant.")

You get the picture. Except it gets worse. One night, for instance, drunk and delirious, I wander out of my apartment to the street and walk around aimlessly, lost. Before long, a CPD car pulls up and two officers approach me. I plaintively and repeatedly shout at them to "Please shoot me!"

They are kind, almost gentle with me. While one explains why they can't shoot me, another calls for an ambulance, which shows up with emergency techs who strap me to a gurney, start an IV and drive me to a hospital where I land in a psychiatric ward.

Perhaps because I was heavily sedated or simply out of my mind, I remember nothing about this psych-ward stay except spending a lot of time in a bed in a dark room with other mad people and a guy at a desk who kept watching us and writing things down. That's it.

Hospital report re: my 2004 "suicide-by-cop" attempt.

## CERTIFICATION REVIEW HEARING REPORT - FRESNO COUNTY

Name of Person Certified: ERIC KRUEGER Medical Record Number: 01-18-03-85

Date of Certification: 10/13/04 MD: ZS/BN Facility: University Medical Center, Unit

Certification Type: [ ] Gravely Disabled [X] Danger to Self [ ] Danger to others

The Following were Present: [X] Person Certified, or [ ] Person waived right to be present. (W&I 5256.3)

Patients' Rights Advocate: K. BOYMANIS Staff: S. KONGBOYAKHAY, MSW

R. YZAGUIRRE, MSWI

The above named person was certified for 14 days of involuntary treatment and the Certification Review Hearing was held on the date below (W & I 5256.4).

[ ] Probable cause exists to detain the person as: [ ] Gravely Disabled [ ] Danger to Self [ ] Danger to Others.

[ ] The person is both willing and able to accept treatment on a voluntary basis (W & I 5250c).

[X] Probable cause does not exist to detain the person.

Reasons for the above determination and evidence relied upon are as follows:

5150: 10/10/04 by CLOVIS PD as: [X] Gravely Disabled [X] Danger to Self [ ] Danger to others

Officer observed ERIC standing on sidewalk, staring at the ground. Later, still there in same position. He said he had no money and was overdrawn at bank and was contemplating stealing food. He said he took a times dosage of his meds prior [illegible]. Only made him groggy. He wanted to kill self but could not do it. He said he wanted officer to kill him with his gun - planned to provoke officer to try. Cert: (Calone) history of Bipolar Dis, PH [illegible] history of progressive depression and chronic suicidality. Currently no psychiatric outpatient care. Dx: Bipolar Dis, depressed. Note: ERIC says Lithium + antidepressant have controlled his Bipolar Dis. since 1978. "I just took a Klonopin." "I always thought if meds don't work, no friends, my writing accepted ... I would take a bottle of Dalmane." ERIC SAID He now rejects that suicide plan and contracted never to suicide. Staff stated that the plan to transfer Eric to a psych hospital was thwarted by CBHC's inability to cope with his intermittent urinary incontinence. Psych staff recommends outpatient psychiatric service.

Person informed of right to a writ: [ ] Requested writ. [ ] Declined writ. [ ] Uncertain. [ ] Unable to understand

Hearing Officer: J.V. Melton LMFT Date: 10/15/04 Time Completed: 12:40 PM

CONFIDENTIAL (California Welfare and Institutions Code 5328) Revised 3-10-2004

I guess I sooner or later calmed down and they let me go home, where all of my weird behavior must have caused my neighbors much consternation and fear because at the end of 2005 the management of my complex evicted me.

# YOU CAN GOOGLE IT

A brief but important sidetrack: If you or a loved one is taking a psychiatric medication, ignore what your shrink does or does not say about the possible side-effects of that medication. Go to a good library and look up your drug in a large volume called the PDR (*Physicians' Desk Reference*)—or "Google" your drug on the Internet and check entries that discuss its possible side-effects.

You see, the shrinks who had me on imipramine for clinical depression either forgot or neglected or were too ill-informed to tell me one of its potential side-effects is major bladder-malfunction; the damn drug over my years of my using it virtually paralyzed my bladder in such a way that it never ever empties, so I—like the guy in the TV commercial—am always going, going, going. (Believe me, this not fun; it can really fuck your quality of life.)

No, not one shrink ever told me this about imipramine. Two urologists did about three years ago. At their urging, I switched to Prozac, which spares the bladder—but nonetheless has a zillion possible side-effects including those I experience such as testicular swelling and pain, bone pain, metabolic disruption, muscle cramps and osteoarthritis. On the good side, for me at least, Prozac delays ejaculation.

Although my urologist, who has run every imaginable bladder test on me, can put me on bladder meds, he'd rather not because I already have three heavy pscyh meds in my body. I have been with him for years, and he believes my bladder is very slowly healing itself now that I'm off imipramine.

I trust him. His problem, and mine, is that these days I'm still having to piss about once an hour, in part due to my bladder but also thanks to my always drinking some kind of fluid: water, diet soda, coffee, lemonade, booze, anything potable; I do this because one of my Prozac side-effects is called "dry mouth." If you've ever smoked grass and experienced what we used to say was "cotton mouth"—well, multiply by 10 and you've got never-ending dry mouth. The only remedy is to drink something, anything, most always.

But please don't get me wrong, my numerous, annoying Prozac side-effects are zip compared to the horrible slow-motion blitzkrieg of major depression.

Overall, my drugs have always worked reasonably well—whenever I was lucky enough to have a psychiatrist who knew how the fuck to manage them. I believe, in addition, that far more efficacious psychopharmacology, relatively free of side-effects, is on the way. Plus I recently heard about experimental brain implants, but I don't have time to Google that.

# A TENACIOUS INFECTION

Sometime during my many visits to my urologist, early 2006, maybe, my lithium level was off the wall, I was drinking heavily and was lost in a dreadfully bad mixed-state when my left eye began to ache quite badly and I ended up, my entire head a mass of pure, high-density pain, as a patient in a downtown-Fresno hospital.

Doctors there told me I had a bacterial infection in my left eye (the source of the bacteria remains unknown). I think they said the infection was so tenacious and powerful I might lose my eye. Given my pre-infection crazed condition, I'm not sure I comprehended what they said, and I don't recall saying anything to them. I later learned they spent the next five days flooding me with antibiotics; and to kill the pain, they put me on a morphine drip (a nice dreamy high). I remember shadows and voices, not much more.

So now we've got my manic-depressive mixed-state, my dangerously infected left eye, my ridiculous bladder, and oh, I forgot, somewhere around this time a surgeon operated on my right foot to fix a number of screwed-up bones that had been forcing me to limp everywhere. And, too, don't ask me how, I lost one of my front teeth; it simply disappeared (did I fall during a blackout?).

At any rate, the hospital's doctors saved my left eye from total destruction, but I ended up blind in that eye. After the hospital, I went to the ophthalmology group I'd been with for years and my specialist there referred me to the group's eye-infection subspecialist (that is, a super-specialist). She spent the next two years treating my infection damage. This included her perfectly replacing my massively scarred cornea with a healthy one from a dead donor, and then, after a long stretch of post-surgical treatment, she removed an infection-spawned cataract that was badly fuzzing my left eye's vision and inserted a prosthetic inner lens. All of these and other steps ultimately restored my savaged eyesight to 20/20 with glasses.

Though I don't believe in miracles, I have always loved and mostly experienced life through my vision, and so, yes, I do consider my return to normal eyesight miraculous. My praise, respect and affection for the physician who pulled it off, Carolyn M. Sakauye, M.D. (her real name), is effusive. And will be until I'm dead, when thanks to an official donor card I carry in my wallet, my organs—especially my corneas—will go to people who need them.

# BAD GUYS

Roughly a year before my half-blindness and during my first year of it, meaning 2004-2006, and still in a horrible, alcoholic, self-destructive manic-depressive mixed-state, I began hanging out with a human subspecies I now call the "Bad Guys."

This label subsumes about a dozen adults, including at least two in their 50s. Some of them either lived in or hung out in a disgusting, broken-down, insect-infested Clovis house owned by an obese, whacko, crippled, shut-in elderly woman who let most anyone crash there and from time to time loaned most anyone money, which, of course, no one ever paid back. Meantime, the house was so derelict Clovis authorities finally ordered the shut-in lady to have it repaired. (Clovis authorities do not want eyesores in a city they proudly call the "Gateway to the Sierras.")

A crazy, promiscuous, vodka-addicted woman I'd met at Ruby's (and had a brief, puke affair with) introduced me to the Bad Guys. I knew they were quintessential losers: woefully alcoholic, subliterate, emotionally arrested at age five, unemployed by choice, ultraparasitic, sexually disturbed and disturbing and, worst of all, compulsively cunning and dishonest, at times criminal. A few were just plain evil.

These physically grown men and women spent most of their time conning each other out of money or outright stealing cash and pawnable property from each other or from trusting relatives, friends and neighbors. Whenever possible, they also ripped-off the state and federal social-service systems.

You see, every one of their twisted days began with their desperate search for money which they almost wholly devoted to buying booze and cigarettes, and junk food when hunger intruded on their collective alcoholic stupor.

Looking back, I think they lived in a near-permanent blackout.

Still, what most troubled me about them was their feeling completely at ease with their sociopathic-psychopathic behavior. In fact, they angrily denied ever doing what sane people and the law would deem wrong. Norman Mailer might have dubbed them "Satan's Children."

And yet I spent—blew—two years hanging out with the Bad Guys. I am fairly certain that during this period I lost what identity I had left; I am fairly certain that my self-esteem on a scale of 100 was -80: I didn't feel worthy of being with anyone better than the Bad Guys; in my mind, I was a wretched, total failure, a mentally ill drunk. So why not hang out with other sicko drunks and losers? These were the kind of people I felt I deserved; and for a time I began to act like them.

During this period, I was somehow always broke. Miserable, desperate and stupid, I let Reggie, a Bad Guy, talk me into Dumpster-diving with him (rummaging through huge garbage bins for plastic and glass bottles and aluminum cans you then take to a recycling place for cash). The Bad Guys called this activity "canning," the meager proceeds of which they devoted to buying 18-packs of Bud Ice beer and arguing over who got how many cans of the shit.

I today can barely believe I did canning for a few months, mostly with Reggie, sometimes alone.

Today, this Bad Guy period is the only part of my life I am still ashamed of. Once I was so broke and so hungry, I actually ate cold, hard discarded pizza I found in someone's Dumpster. What a fucking nightmare.

But the absolute worst came when a so-called friend of Reggie's, a real idiot fulltime-scavenger-thief-beggar, convinced me—I was crazed, penniless and smoking cigarette butts I found in the street—to hang outside a liquor store with him and panhandle its entering and exiting customers. I did this for about 15 minutes, then, despite my madness and half-blindness and aching foot and acute hunger, I luckily, vividly realized that I did not spend six hard years in college and so many years of writing to be a beggar. I went home. I don't remember what I did there aside from thinking heavily about suicide.

o o o

My eviction came shortly after the beggar thing, and at the start of 2006 I found a new apartment in the only poor, multiracial, multiethnic neighborhood I know of in Clovis. At this point, my life and my mental state were very slowly changing for the better. And when some of the Bad Guys started hanging out at my new place, I forget how, but I soon got them to stop coming over.

The one exception was Reggie, whom I insanely considered a friend and thus insanely allowed him to spend countless days and nights at my place. He turned out to be the most manipulative, lying, thieving, delusional, toxic person I'd ever known in or out of a mental hospital—he was also confused about his sexuality, in that he posed as this big tough manly guy and had a girlfriend but most every day under his jeans wore women's panties and at times a matching bra. He insisted on calling his anus his "pussy," and he loved to have other men lick it and fuck him up the ass.

I'm ashamed to confess that despite my lifelong heterosexuality I was one of the guys who, for a short spell, pleasured Reggie. Honestly not sure why. And although I was in a partial or total alcoholic blackout when I did this, I still have some dark, blurred, ugly, cold mental images of having my dick inside him and never ejaculating. These images haunt me.

Oh well, I finally, thanks to some sanity and with great urgency, told Reggie to hook up with gay guys because I was into women, not men, and would no longer fuck him. He complied, saying maybe I'd change my mind one day. Never did—but he kept coming over, often unannounced, and when he wasn't doing that he was phoning me up to five times a day to see where I was and what I was doing.

Now, I'd seen and heard Reggie use my phone to stalk other people, but I needed time to realize I was one of his targets: That did it, in late 2006, my sanity returning, I decided I wanted this sick bastard out of my life for good. In turn, I halted all phone communications with him, never picking up if I heard his con-artist crap whining from my answering machine. And when he sometimes popped up at my door, banging on it, pleading with me or angrily ordering me to admit him, I never let him in, or even acknowledged his presence. He'd eventually leave and I'd go back to whatever I was doing.

But when he popped up banging on my door in June 2007—I'd by this time kept him totally severed from my life for six months—I furiously decided I was either going to kill him (a "rage" killing) or call the Clovis police. Good for me: I called 9-1-1, summarized the sick situation. As I was talking to the emergency operator, who must have sent out some kind of officer-needed signal, Reggie abruptly left my door and headed to the street, where three Clovis black-and-whites cornered him. One officer cell-phoned me from the scene, told me what was happening, said if Reggie ever came near me again, I should call CPD and report an "unwanted person" and they'd throw him in jail.

I guess the police made an impression on Reggie because he made a fast and total exit from my life. And my life steadily bettered. Whew.

o o o

By the way, I know Reggie and the other Bad Guys need intensive psychiatric help. On the other hand, I recall the numerous times I gently advised Reggie to get some sort of psychotherapy. He'd emphatically retort he was sane, the problem was other people—and the universe.

Hey, I've got my own madness to deal with. So fuck him and all the other Bad Guys.

# *"IT HAS A CALMIMG EFFECT"*

Latif Ziyar, M.D.

Please let me digress to tell you about Latif Ziyar (his real name) M.D., my psychiatrist for the last three years. A psychiatric hospital referred me to him for outpatient care after I'd been acutely suicidal in late 2005. I saw him monthly and now bimonthly for medication management and brief talks about how I'm doing overall.

Dr. Ziyar truly knows manic-depression. And what makes him so important to me thus far is that after my first long interview with him, he kept me on Prozac and Klonopin, but took me off lithium and put me on generic Neurontin (gapapentin), an anti-epilepsy drug some shrinks are now using to treat clinical mania.

He told me Neurontin had a "calming effect," didn't require monthly blood tests and didn't have lithium's unpleasant side-effects, like my awful, constant and clearly visible and embarrassing hand tremor.

Given the tremor, plus lithium's scary instability, plus my having more than once shot up through it into manic episodes, I gladly switched to Neurontin. And for me, at least, it works far better than lithium. What I call the "psychology" of my manic-depression (for example, perceiving the world in black and white, no shades of gray), and my numerous acquired neuroses (like projection and transference) are still in place. Nonetheless, I have rarely if ever felt so relatively stable. And the fucking tremor is gone!

I've Googled Neurontin and found nobody seems to know precisely how it suppresses mania, but it does. And its side-effects in my case are minimal: occasional drowsiness and forgetfulness, and at times a mild tingling throughout my body. One nice side-effect is heightened libido; these days I can look at a pretty woman for a nanosecond and get aroused. Dr. Ziyar told me other patients had reported this. He also noted with a smile that this side-effect, combined with Prozac's delayed ejaculation, "lets you stay harder longer."

Neurontin's only enemy is alcohol. If have more than six hard-liquor drinks in one evening, I run the risk of bursting through my Neurontin barrier and for a few hours experiencing a manic episode, which means I'm prone to doing something stupid and self-destructive, like ending up at a blackjack table and losing money I can not afford to lose—as I did one night in May 2007 during an alcohol-induced mini-mania, despite my being on 1,200 mg/day of Neurontin.

The morning after the gambling episode, I was sober, stable and so alarmed by what I'd done that I doubled my Neurontin dose to 2,400mg/day and told Dr. Ziyar what had happened. He agreed with my new dose, and I was fine until August. That's when I went to New Jersey to celebrate with my father his 87th birthday, and briefly snapped into a father-induced rage-mania. I've had no manic episodes in the year since, and now my Neurontin is down to 1,600 mg/day.

Meantime, I do my best to strictly regulate my drinking. Dr. Ziyar at some point during every session we have urges me to stop drinking altogether. He says that with Neurontin and my other meds, I don't need alcohol. I essentially tell him I will continue to drink but will try to cut down. He tells me that taking my bedtime Neurontin on top of alcohol could mean I may"never wake up." I tell him I've been mixing meds and booze for 30 years, and I silently wonder how much Neurontin and how much alcohol I'd need to deliberately kill myself:

Even now, with my life so rich with people and experience, I sometimes think about suicide. Remember, my meds control manic-depression, but they do not exorcize it. To date, nothing does.

# LIFE WITH FATHER: THE SEQUEL

Back to that most recent manic episode in New Jersey: My father and I have been at war with each other for more than 45 years, that is, ever since I first said "No" to him. Against each other we have variously waged hot war, cold war, guerilla war, covert operations, hand-to-hand combat, psychological war, espionage and more.

And yet we both at times over those many years have tried and succeeded to connect, at least for a few moments, minutes, once in a while a few hours.

And remember, I am now 58 and still searching for, arguably craving, the loving father I never had.

Psychiatrist-psychotherapist Fritz Perls might shout at me something like "What do you need your father for? Throw him in the garbage can!"

I'm not there yet. Maybe I'll never be. I certainly wasn't there in late 2006 and the first seven months of 2007 when my father and I enjoyed relatively good long-distance phone discussions about books, theater, film, TV, politics, family events and more. Fact is, I actually thought we were finally making genuine contact, finally growing closer; I felt he finally respected me as an autonomous adult male and a writer, despite my crazy past and our countless fights.

In my optimism about our relationship, I arranged in July 2007 to fly from California to New Jersey, where I would spend 10 days with him in Long Branch at his summer condo right on the Atlantic Ocean (his winter condo is in affluent Chatham, N.J.)—and with him celebrate on August 3rd his 87th birthday.

I was so taken by the notion of our having a terrific time together that I spent a lot of time writing the following birthday card for my dad. Here's the text:

**August 3, 2007**

***HAPPY***

***BIRTHDAY***

***DAD!!!***

**Dear Dad,**

**Since I can't afford to buy you the kind of birthday present I'd like you to have for your 87th birthday, I've assembled below some of your words not in my published newspaper work—words you said to me over the past 50+ years.**

**Words still alive in me.**

1. *"Let's see. On December 7, 1941, I was in Puerto Rico sunning myself on a raft in the ocean when someone swam out and yelled Pearl Harbor had been attacked. I'd never heard of Pearl Harbor. But I got my draft notice a few weeks later."*

2. *"You'll never work this hard in college."*

**Remember: You told me this past midnight when I was a high-school freshman killing myself over that stupid research paper about the Aztecs.**

3. *"Eric, come here, look at this."*

**Remember, too: You said this before showing childhood me that 1945 U.S. Army report about Dachau and the Holocaust.**

4. **That summer when, with Mom, El** [my special nickname for my sister Ellen] **and me in tow, you were studying at the University of Vermont; one day you got a letter saying you received a B for in one of your courses. "You got a B?" I asked, puzzled, disappointed (you were a teacher, after all). "Too bad you didn't get an A."**

**You looked at me surprised and asked,** *"What's wrong with a B?"*

**I wish I'd remembered your rhetorical query during those painful times in high school and college when I was so desperate for sky-high grades—and got them —only to find when I entered the job market that they were worthless.**

5. *"You should have been a Ph.D., a university professor of English."*

**No, the Ph.D. is a research degree and too many professors at too many colleges care far more about their research and publishing than about teaching, which they consider a regrettable chore that comes with the Mount Olympus of scholarship.**

**(By contrast, you and El, with your "lowly" M.A.s, are avatars of stellar classroom teaching. I am proud of that.)**

*6. "Sometimes I ask myself, did I really spend 3½ years in the Army—in World War II?"*

**You did.**

7. *"When I went back to Columbia to finish my doctorate, they said I'd been gone too long and all the credits I'd earned earlier had been wiped out. I was working, I had a family, I couldn't bear starting over again, so I didn't."*

**That may have been a mitzvah.**

*8. "You're depressing the whole family."*

**You told me this when I was a sophomore at Livingston, home for a weekend, and into my eighth month of clinical depression.**

**You were right. I later learned from therapy and books that manic-depressives like me, when insanely up or down, profoundly scare, sadden or hurt the people around them, especially the people who most care about them.**

9. *"We didn't know we were poor. Everyone was poor."*

**So along with World War II, you also made it through the Great Depression. No wonder Brokaw calls your generation "The Greatest."**

10. **I still ask you about your WWII years, and you answer with rich anecdotes—and sometimes (for me at least) thrilling snippets like:** *"I saw Patton at a party... I saw Sinatra... My office was down the hall from William Wyler's... I flew to France on D+20... We threw Germans out of their homes so our officers could have them."*

11. *"It's okay to come home on weekends. President Kennedy loved to spend his weekends on Martha's Vineyard."*

**I was clinically depressed my first year at NYU, and you thought my getting away from school would help me. I thought it was a sign of weakness. I was wrong and luckily followed your advice; and, yes, I grew happier with each visit.**

12. **Earlier that same year (Thanksgiving weekend, 1968, to be precise), I was miserably writer-blocked on a term paper for Modern European History. You urged me to** *"Stop worrying and get it down on paper."*

**I did. I even got an A for my effort. And I replayed your words five years later while pushing to finish my Master's thesis (hence its dedication to you).**

**From then till now, whenever I freeze and can't get the words out, I hear your advice, and what I want to get on paper ultimately gets there. So thanks.**

**I could list much more but I'll stop, only adding that I owe you big time for my current run of relatively good mental health and for what material joys I have, like my Granada apartment and the new Dell computer I'm writing this on and the plane ticket that brought me here.**

**Here, to your condo on the mesmeric Atlantic.**

**Here, to celebrate your birthday, with love.**

[signed Eric]

o o o

So now I have just spent five days at my father's oceanfront condo. I am 57; he is 87. This is August 2007, but from the start the year is not 2007, the year to me feels somewhere around 1958 during one of those million times when in his demented mind I am his rotten kid.

Result: He is his same old warped and warping control-freak self with me. I'm doing my best to be nice, to deflect his negative comments about me, to connect with him, to keep the peace. But even my daily 40 mg of Prozac, .5 mg of Klonopin and 2,400 mg of Neurontin, plus alcohol, aren't helping me in the face of his twisted words and behavior. Here are but a few of his remarks to me (I wrote them down minutes after he made them):

1.He barks at or criticizes or questions or undercuts whatever I do every waking hour I am with him. He only stops when I get him to talk about his World War II years or his Great Depression youth of poverty.

2. He says to me more than once, "You have to obey me, whether you like it or not."

3. He says to me more than once, "This is my house. You have to obey my rules."

4. One morning he orders me to fold two bath towels and tells me exactly how to do so and exactly where and how to place them. I gently try to remind him I've been folding towels on my own for 35 years; he keeps giving me orders about the towels; he doesn't hear me. In fact, he never once hears me during my oceanfront time with him.

5."Eric, don't put paper towels in the toilet bowl," my father shouts at me.

I answer: "No. I never do that."

Father: "I know. Just a reminder."

6. Here's the deal-breaker: He and I are sitting on his terrace and out of nowhere he says regarding my chair, "Your chair is dusty."

Me: "I don't care."

Him: "Yes, you do care."

No surprise I only lasted five days with him. You see, when he tells me on the terrace that I care about the chair—after all the shit I've taken from him—he finally overwhelms all of my defenses and hits my manic-rage button: I grab his arm and scream over and over "I will kill you in two seconds with one hand if you don't shut up."I am serious, I will do it, I will smash his trachea, and I enjoy seeing the fear in his fucking eyes. I will no longer tolerate him treating me like a child-slave, I will annihilate him and his control-mad, crazymaking, paranoid, toxic, psychotic behavior.

o o o

I didn't smash his trachea. I went to a bar and then to my sister's place for the night. I returned here to Clovis the next morning. I was at peace again.

o o o

Détente came a few months later, as usual, and my father and I are once again talking weekly and amiably on the phone.

Once in a while, however, he regresses into control-nonsense like: "You should have been a Ph.D., a university professor of English."

No, I remind him, I never after age 12 wanted a Ph.D. and a professorship; I remind him I kept changing my career goals almost every year; I remind him I never knew what I wanted to do with my life, save that by my late teens I wanted to be some kind of writer.

I remind him. But I never get through; he is wrapped in Kevlar, deflecting my words and charging on with stuff about the joys of teaching and what a great teacher of composition I would have made—and could today, at a community college since I have a Master's. I am 58, and he still doesn't hear me.

When he starts telling me what I should and should not do in my daily life, I change the topic. When he gets his weird kicks by reminding me of horrible things I did to him in the past, I answer his punitive words with false contrition or simply gaze out my window at the palm trees and the soft blue sky of the Central Valley, and, when necessary, when my meds can no longer block him, I pour drinks while he talks, and I drift away. Booze is my last defense against his madness. Once drinking, I don't hear him.

When I don't need to block his words, we have fine discussions. We even enjoy gossiping about other members of our large extended family: Who is a real schmuck? Which of our cousins is gay or lesbian? Why is one relative on his fourth wife? Who had a fight with whom? And so on. It's fun. We laugh and pepper our talk with Yiddish words like mishegas, zaftig, shmatte, metsieh.

And, I admit, he does his best to avoid our "hot topics," the ones that spark our arguments—topics like my heavy drinking, my smoking, my abject failure to handle money well.

Absent firefights over my behavior, we enjoy each other.

o o o

Since the start of 2006, perhaps much earlier, my father, perhaps out of guilt or some need to prove to himself and the world that he loves me no matter what, has paid my rent, my cable TV and my meds.

I don't know exactly why he helps me.

I do know that asking him would not necessarily produce a useful or verifiable answer.

In any case, I call his money"reparations": compensation for the damage he did me in the past. My sister thinks my talking about reparations is total bullshit. She says my father helps me because he "believes in" my writing. Maybe she's right.

# CLOVIS

I spent time with good friends these days, most of them also my neighbors. I confess I still worry about my behavior when with them, still have to fight off projection and transference and other neuroses. But at the same time I feel these people accept me as very few people in my life ever have. They don't criticize me, don't try to change or control me. In turn, the high degree of comfort I feel when interacting with them I've only experienced a few times in my entire life.

Perhaps what pleases me most is that I have shared with these people my psychiatric history and they don't seem to care. As my friend and neighbor John says, "Hey, we've all got problems."

o o o

I walk up Villa Avenue in Clovis most every day to shop at Wal*Mart and MG Liquor. And most every day, in one way or another, from a quick silent eye-lock to a 30-minute conversation about Iraq, I interact with all kinds of human beings. I call them my "Street People." These are folks I don't really know but somehow do know. I enjoy them and feel good when we connect. Among them are the warm, crazy guy who has trouble pronouncing words but manages to ask me for a cigarette, tells me he prays for me, hugs me and wanders off; the woman in the scooter who is missing a leg and waves and yells out "Hi Eric!" as she zips past me at the busy intersection of Villa and Shaw; the benign but clearly troubled guy who's pacing down Villa and angrily arguing aloud with someone who's not there; the many young mothers and fathers—Hispanic, Asian, Pakistani, Indian, black, white—pushing babies in carriages or holding the hands of bouncing toddlers; the huge black guy sitting on his huge black Harley with the bike's built-in stereo blaring. I smile at him and say, "Nice bike." He smiles and says "Thanks." I could go on for pages, but I think you get the picture.

Still, let me add the following strange but not unusual interaction:

This is the morning of September 4, 2007, I am walking on the sidewalk along Villa to MG Liquor when a bare-chested, age-60ish, heavily tattooed, big white guy walking a tiny poodle 30 feet away shouts out to me, "Hey you're looking good, much better!"

I wonder to myself, "Better then when? And who is this guy? Did I meet him years ago in some bar? On the street?" While I scan my memory, he keeps shouting and smiling but I can't hear him above all the traffic noise on Villa.

Then the traffic dies down and I hear him say, "You know, I look out for you."

I smile and thank him for looking out for me.

Then he repeats, "You look much better." Only this time he asks, "Bipolar? Bipolar?

I smile, "Yeah, 40 years."

He next reminds me, twice, to take my meds. I assure him I am taking my meds. After this, the traffic noise picks up and we happily shout to each other, "Take care!" and walk away in opposite directions.

When I walk into MG Liquor a few moments later, I am talking aloud to myself about this encounter and laughing, but then I abruptly shut up, worried the people in the store will think I'm crazy.

o o o

Between my street-people interactions and Wal*Mart (one of my friends calls the experience of shopping there "field anthropology") and all the fascinating sights and sounds of the streets and my brain processing all this stuff—I live in what astrophysicist Neil Tyson might label a "neuro-multiverse."

Unfortunately, this realm includes my fights with periodic spurts of neurosis. Exhibit A: paranoid projection. While walking around Clovis, I often see cops driving by and I instantly, fearfully assume they are watching me from their vehicles with great suspicion. Then red flashing neon lights go off in my mind, and I firmly tell myself that I am projecting: I am looking at the cops; I don't have a clue as to what they're looking at or thinking or feeling. To back this up, I summon the "uncertainty principle"—from a brilliant guy named Heisenberg—which to me means we can't be absolutely certain about anything, and about that we can't be absolutely certain.

o o o

Sometimes I fantasize about returning to L.A. or moving to Berlin or some other big, exciting, faraway city. But then I realize that Clovis, like Livingston College, takes care of me, cradles me. Perhaps Clovis is the perfect place for people like me. Perhaps that's why I stay here.

# FINDING THE CRUISE CONTROL

I recently saw a reporter on CNN interview a Marine who'd come back from Iraq with both legs gone and shrapnel in his skull, a Marine who ended the story of his war injuries by saying with a slight shrug, a hint of resignation mixed with resolve, and a smile, "So I live with it."

Walking home from Wal*Mart and MG Liquor the next morning, I realized this applies to me and my manic-depression. You see, over the past five years, I've been feeling for the most part happy, alive, at times stoned on reality. But my meds are the only barrier between me and insanity.

And just as I can never know for sure when or if an asteroid the size of Texas will blow up the Earth or a tiny blood clot will shut down my brain—I can never know with absolute certainty when or if, despite my meds, I will cross the line again and spiral up or down into madness.

I live with this not knowing. And I try to have fun. Like the wounded soldier I saw on CNN. He was wearing a T-shirt that read, "Marine for sale. Partial assembly required."

LaVergne, TN USA
14 February 2011
216494LV00005B/224/P

9 781451 213508